CW00816428

ONE OF THESE
FINE DAYS

Myfanwy, 1914

MYFANWY THOMAS

ONE OF THESE
FINE DAYS
—memoirs—

Drawings by Henry Croly

CARCANET NEW PRESS / MANCHESTER
with
Mid Northumberland Arts Group

First published in Great Britain 1982
by Carcanet New Press Limited
330 Corn Exchange Buildings
Manchester M4 3BG
with
Mid Northumberland Arts Group
Town Hall, Station Road, Ashington, Northumberland

Second Impression 1982

SBN 85635 3876 (Carcanet)
SBN 0 904790 231 (MidNAG)

The publisher acknowledges the financial assistance
of the Arts Council of Great Britain.

Printed in England by Short Run Press Ltd., Exeter

CONTENTS

Acknowledgments

The author would like to thank the Oxford University Press for permission to print poems from *The Collected Poems of Edward Thomas*, edited by George Thomas (1978); and the Estate of Robert Frost, the editor, Edward Connery Latham, and Jonathan Cape Ltd, for permission to print 'To E. T.' and 'Iris by Night' from *The Poetry of Robert Frost*.

To our parents
Helen and Edward
with their children
grandchildren
and nine great-grandchildren

ONE OF THESE FINE DAYS

ANOTHER GIRL

ON 26 December 1909 Edward Thomas wrote to his friend Jesse Berridge: 'Both children were at Bedales last term as Helen was teaching there, but I don't know if Bronwen will manage the longer walk next term especially as Helen may be unable to teach—she is going to have another baby in the summer.'

On 15 March 1910 he mentions to Jesse: 'Helen is very well indeed and has been teaching at school again this term.'

And on 26 August 1910: 'I am sorry I did not write. Helen addressed a lot of postcards to send out after the event and did not do one for you and so I forgot too. It was 9 days ago now, another girl I am glad to say, and Helen and she have done very well from the start though the birth itself was a laborious one.'

And later in December of that year: 'Helen is nearly as well as ever now—not quite. The baby is Helen Elizabeth Myfanwy. I must tell you how to say Myfanwy, tho quite easy and obvious if you are not frightened by the look of it. She is very well and bright.'

After being in labour for two weary days and nights, as the sun rose on a hazy August morning Helen Thomas was at last safely delivered of a ten-pound daughter. Mother and child were exhausted, bruised and torn by the long struggle of parting. Helen had expected a boy, but Edward wanted a second daughter; after much thought and consulting the *Mabinogion*, pondering on Olwen, discarding Blodwen as being too much like Bronwen, their second child's name, he chose Myfanwy, Helen, after his wife, and Elizabeth, his mother's second name; her first name, Mary, had been given to Bronwen.

At the age of thirty-one Edward Thomas was an established
writer of essays, of books on the English country and of
biographies, and also a literary critic of some reputation. In
1909 with his wife Helen and their two children, Merfyn
born in 1900 and Bronwen in 1902, he moved in late autumn
to the house where I was born the following summer. Three
years earlier they had moved from Kent to Berryfield
Cottage, a mile or so from the village of Steep, near Peters-
field, Hampshire, in order that the two children could go
daily to Bedales, a co-educational boarding school founded
early in the century. The school had high ideals in art and
literature, and in general living, expressed in its motto,
'Work of each for weal of all'. Lessons and other activities in
the open air were encouraged. Merfyn and Bronwen's con-
temporaries included John Rothenstein, who later became
Director of the Tate Gallery; Ramsay MacDonald's son Mal-
colm; Konni Zilliacus, MP; John Wyndham, creator of *The
Triffids*; Edward Barnsley, furniture maker; Julia Strachey;
and many others who were to become distinguished in art
and politics. There was no religious instruction. Helen
helped in the preparatory school, Dunhurst.

The new house, built for Edward and Helen by Geoffrey
Lupton, stood high above Berryfield, which lay at the foot
of the steep downland called the Shoulder of Mutton. The
house had no name then but stood with two or three others
in Cockshott Lane in the parish of Froxfield; Edward
headed his letters either 'Week Green' or, more often, 'Wick
Green'. The terraced garden sloped down towards the great
hanger of yew, beech, ash and wild cherry, often hidden in
mist; and after a rainstorm plumes of smoke-like vapour
would suddenly rise from the layers of trees. It was a large
house, built sturdily from oak timbers and seasoned red
brick. The floor of the long living-room was made from
planks taken from a barn threshing-floor, three or four

inches thick and polished to a soft pewter colour by the
flails which had beaten out the grain from hundreds of har-
vests, and from the sliding movements of the ash-wood
shovels used to fill the sacks with corn. Most of the windows
looked on to a wide brick terrace which ran along the garden
side of the house; a curved niche in the kitchen wall near
the oven made a sunny, warm place for Helen to sit making
baby clothes with minute tucks, lace edgings, and tiny
buttonholes. Surrounded by the soothing scent of lavender,
bergamot, sage, rue and southernwood, and the dreamy hum
of Lupton's bees ravishing the flowers. In the distance lay
Berryfield and the village of Steep, and beyond, the great
ridge of the South Downs. Edward did his writing in Geoffrey
Lupton's Bee House, half of which was adapted for use as a
study.

Merfyn was delighted with the new baby, Bronwen a little
scornful: 'You think yourself so proper now you've got that
baby.'

The Michaelmas term at the school had begun by the
time the monthly nurse had left; Helen, still a little weak
from the long labour, was advised by the doctor to go for
occasional airings in an open Victoria carriage.

Bronwen and Merfyn went daily to the junior school,
walking and running down the steep Old Stoner Hill, using
the path Edward was to recall in the spring of 1915:

> Running along a bank, a parapet
> That saves from the precipitous wood below
> The level road, there is a path. It serves
> Children for looking down the long smooth steep,
> Between the legs of beech and yew, to where
> A fallen tree checks the sight: while men and women
> Content themselves with the road and what they see
> Over the bank, and what the children tell.

The path, winding like silver, trickles on,
Bordered and even invaded by thinnest moss
That tries to cover roots and crumbling chalk
With gold, olive, and emerald, but in vain.
The children wear it. They have flattened the bank
On top, and silvered it between the moss
With the current of their feet, year after year.
But the road is houseless, and leads not to school.
To see a child is rare there, and the eye
Has but the road, the wood that overhangs
And underyawns it, and the path that looks
As if it led on to some legendary
Or fancied place where men have wished to go
And stay; till, sudden, it ends where the wood ends.

My earliest memory of my father is of sitting astride his
foot, with him holding my hands and waving his leg up and
down, higher and higher, until that delicious gasping moment
when he let go my hands and I flew through the air into
his arms.

> This is the way the farmer rides,
> Hobble-de-hoy, hobble-de-hoy;
> This is the way the lady rides,
> Nimminy-nim, nimminy-nim;
> This is the way the gentleman rides,
> Trit-trot, trit-trot;
> And this is the way the huntsman rides,
> A-gallop, a-gallop, a-gallop
> And TUMBLES into the ditch!

My mother's face and person, particularly the touch of
her strong, firm hands, I knew well: my attachment to her
filled my being. She had held me close so often since my
birth, near enough for me to see and absorb her presence

with my dull-sighted eyes. Everything more than a yard or two from me must have been hazy and indistinct, and I needed to be near those I loved and depended upon. It was a particular pleasure to be on my father's knee, wrapped in a blanket after being bathed, while he sang in Welsh, or my favourite 'Oh father, father, come build me a boat', or the sea shanties he had learned from Marston, one of the crew from Shackleton's Polar expedition—because then I could see his face clearly, admire his curling hair, and catch a glimpse of his gold tooth. This, I thought, must be his 'sweet tooth' which Mother and Bronwen teased him about.

In the early morning I enjoyed the warm, close world of the blanket fronds on the fold of bedclothes in my parents' bed, while they dressed and sipped early morning tea. Sometimes I was given a saucer of milk with a dash of tea for a treat, and when I had sipped it, I would watch the procession of tiny shapes close to my eyes, made by the upstanding wool which moved when I gently blew and changed their outlines.

Later, when I had come to know the room and its furniture and pictures intimately, I was fascinated by the portrait of Shelley, with his delicate, rather girlish features and long curling hair. Death was a mysterious subject, towards which I sometimes tried to steer the talk, while blowing gently on the procession of tiny figures on my horizon.

'Wouldn't it be lovely if we could see all the dead people in the churchyard.'

'I don't think it would at all.'

'Why?'

'I'm rather tired of this talk about dead people.'

'Do you know any?'

Impatiently, 'No.'

'Oh you *do*—you know Shelley and Rags.' Rags was the sheep-dog which had been a beloved companion. He and I

had often been found curled up asleep together, with me
sucking the silky tip of his ear.

Bronwen was a contented, self-contained little girl,
cheeking her father if he seemed stern, happy to wander the
lanes picking wild-flowers and learning their names from
him, or sitting on the terrace making tiny doll's-clothes for
her cupie doll. Once she left her sewing in the garden while
she came indoors for lunch; afterwards, several of the tiny
garments were missing. She hunted among the lavender
bushes where the wind might have blown them. Months later
she found a robin's nest in the toolshed, carefully lined with
the missing clothes. Only occasionally did Bronwen have
black moods; during one she growled in her deep voice: 'I
hate Mummy, I hate Daddy, I hate Edith, I hate Merfyn, I
hate Rags and I hate the baby.' I remember our gentle cousin
Margaret saying in a shocked voice, 'Fancy hating *Rags*!'

With her corn-coloured hair, large brown eyes and russet
cheeks, Bronwen was a great favourite with visitors to the
house. Ralph Hodgson, who gave her a splendid bull-terrier
called Dinah, had her on his knee one day and was flirting
with her. My father, puritanical in many ways, expostulated:
'She *is* only eight, Hodgson.' 'That's nothing to what I'd
do if she were eighteen!' he replied with a great roar of
laughter. Dinah was a much-loved creature and was gentle
and biddable with the family, but extremely fierce to tradesmen; they refused to call on her account so my father had
to find another home for her. Ralph Hodgson was deeply
hurt and for a long time avoided coming to the house.

Mother would take me out in a wooden push-chair called
a mail-cart, along the lanes or down the long hill to Steep.
Sometimes we were given a ride in Mrs Dennet's pony trap,
from which she delivered pats of dewy butter wrapped in a
fresh cabbage leaf, and brown eggs from a large basket.
Often we would picnic on the Shoulder of Mutton among

the juniper bushes and yew-trees, while Bronwen picked bunches of harebells, milkwort and sheeps-bit scabious. If my father were with us he would swing me up on his shoulders, one stubby leg either side of his neck, and grasping my ankles while I clenched my fists in his curly hair, he would gallop down the slope, I catching my breath with joyous fear as the wind rushed by my ears. The picnic knife for cutting the fruit-cake, of which my father was so fond, was cleaned by digging the blade into the springy turf, apple-cores were hidden in bushes and wrapping papers put back into the haversack.

The exciting terror of bounding down the Mutton on my father's shoulders was quite different from the fear I felt when I clambered up the stairs, looking for my mother who was resting; Edith would bundle me in her arms, telling me that Mother had 'gone for a soldier'.

While we lived at Wick Green, I don't remember many people outside the immediate family. But I vividly recall a visit with Mother to an elderly childless couple who also lived in Cockshott Lane. The husband, a timid, quiet man, had the unusual Christian name of Amphlet. At lunch I found a long hair in my custard—the first time this had happened—and I felt my gorge rise and to Mother's consternation and our hostess's irritation, I could eat no more and had to try and look anywhere but at the disgusting plate before me. At tea, the gingerbread was burnt, so not only did the ginger burn my tongue, but the black charred sides were dry and bitter and I could scarcely swallow my first mouthful; although it was forbidden, I had to take a gulp of milk to wash it down. I could eat no more. 'It *is* rather hot, my dear,' ventured Amphlet, and I felt grateful for this comment in an otherwise disapproving atmosphere.

The strange hazy world of short-sight which I lived in for my first four years made me extra-dependent upon my mother, and I felt insecure when she was out of the house. My peering eyes and left-handedness made me clumsy; I dropped cups when helping to lay the tea-things, I bumped into furniture and tripped over steps. My father would say I had two left hands, and called me 'scrammy-handed'. My short-sightedness was first noticed on the day when he called us into the garden to see a hoopoe sitting on the fence with its crest spread. My screwed-up eyes and tears of frustration at being unable to share the excitement made my parents realise that all I could see was a fuzzy blob. So I was taken to an oculist in Portsmouth; small wire-rimmed spectacles soon opened up a new world for me. But although I have worn glasses all my life and with their help can see perfectly well, I am clumsy and still have two left hands. And I have never seen a hoopoe.

Edward must have had some pleasant times up at Wick Green, with Geoffrey Lupton in his workshop, though there is no mention in any of his letters of the considerable number of hours he must have spent there learning to be a passably skilful carpenter. He made himself a circular-topped three-legged table and when working late he used a candle with a polished reflector which seemed to burn very slowly and give a soft light. He made a large blanket-chest with big handmade nails down the sides, a three-legged stool—perhaps for me. It was apt to tip over and is now made steady with a circle of plywood screwed to the legs. And, choicest of all, a hand-wrought—perhaps by *his* hands—iron-banded oak deed-box. All are still in constant use. How he must have enjoyed working with good sharp tools, choosing his wood from the neatly stacked piles in Lupton's store—sawing, chiselling, chamfering, hammering and finally polishing with wax from Lupton's own bees. He made book-shelves, too, which he kept in the Bee House for his reference books and review copies; and in this study he stuck on the walls various posters which amused him—one for an indigestion mixture had printed in bold type at the top,

SPRING IS COMING!
BRINGING DEBILITY

But the house where I was born—indeed, mine was the first birth it had known—was one in which my parents were never at ease. The mists, the wind and the flinty earth of the garden depressed my father's restless spirit, and at last the family moved down into the village of Steep to one of six semi-detached workmen's cottages.

The poem 'Wind and Mist' was written on 1 April 1915, not long after we had moved from the house down to the small cottage. In it the poet has a long conversation with a stranger who is admiring the house:

'. . . Doubtless the house was not to blame,
But the eye watching from those windows saw,
Many a day, day after day, mist—mist
Like chaos surging back—and felt itself
Alone in all the world, marooned alone.
We lived in clouds, on a cliff's edge almost
(You see), and if clouds went, the visible earth
Lay too far off beneath and like a cloud.
I did not know it was the earth I loved
Until I tried to live there in the clouds
And the earth turned to cloud.'
                                    'You had a garden
Of flint and clay, too.' 'True; that was real enough.
The flint was the one crop that never failed.
The clay first broke my heart, and then my back;
And the back heals not. There were other things

Real, too. In that room at the gable a child
Was born while the wind chilled a summer dawn:
Never looked grey mind on a greyer one
Than when the child's cry broke above the groans.'
'I hope they were both spared.' 'They were. Oh yes.
But flint and clay and childbirth were too real
For this cloud castle. I had forgot the wind.
Pray do not let me get on to the wind.
You would not understand about the wind . . .'

FAMILY

THE family circle—grandparents, aunts, uncles and cousins—
was an important part of our lives, even though a long time
often passed between visits to and from them.

I never met mother's parents, James Ashcroft Noble and
Esther. Grandfather Noble died in 1896, a gentle man, much
loved by both Helen and Edward. Edward had been greatly
helped by Grandfather Noble and dedicated his first published book, *The Woodland Life*, to him. Edward wrote this
letter to him on the eve of publication, but sadly Mr Noble
died a few hours before the postman arrived, on Good
Friday, 3 April 1896. Edward was then aged eighteen years
and one month.

Postmarked *Wandsworth S.W. 3 p.m.*
Ap 2 96

61 Shelgate Road
Battersea Rise

My dear Mr Noble,

It is not the happiness—can it be the inexperience or
lightness?—of youth, which makes a storm, calm though
it be, a dream. Though I *am light* the thought troubles me.

Could this letter reach you able and ready to read it, I
would try and tell you what I have been thinking; though
I once told you I cried because I was incapable of thought.

But though the present seems a dream, I can look back
on our friendship and its bright reality and truth as indeed
no dream; unless that, too, is one of those fairy touches
that we feel in sleep.

This is no time for thanks, but perhaps now and then
you have recollected our gone letters and talks; then you
will feel that your good influence and help has sometimes
drawn me from the enwrapping pleasure of scenes which

before held me alone with them. At Swindon in the
stillness of birdsong when I tried to meditate, I wandered
back to the time when with your surpassing kindness and
insight you made ways clear which before had been dark
or fearful with doubt. I can not say more plainly what I
mean, but at any time a word would recall how you
helped me in my passes of life. You who have lived a life
will know, as none who do not know me can know, what
you have been to me. You have brought light where
there was uncertainty; you have shown me what I knew
not; perhaps in part you have made me know myself,
understood before by you.

I cannot say goodbye. I cannot hope; I can almost
wish that it, that all, will pass in dream. If only my silly
simple words could swing a breath of pureness and health
like the violets I might rest.

In life, your affectionate and grateful friend
EDWY THOMAS

Helen wrote to Janet Hooton on 6 January 1907:

Berryfield Cottage

My dear Janet

I've just had a letter from Irene, saying that Mother
died on Friday afternoon. I expect you knew she had
been ill for three weeks, with what was thought to be
ulcerated stomach. I saw her for the day last Monday,
and tho very weak and fragile, she was mending the
doctor said, after a dangerous two days. On Friday she
seemed better than ever, when some complication in the
throat occurred, and she died with only poor little Mary
with her, I believe, Irene scouring the neighbourhood for
a doctor.

It's all very sudden and terrible. Mother was so well

and jolly when she helped me move here, and death
seemed so very far away. I am not going to the funeral.
It is 2.30 on Monday. So now we've got neither Mother
nor Father, and there's a dreadful gap made. I don't
know what Lance will do. I thought I'd let you know, as
Irene might not think of writing in all the hurry and
bewilderment that death causes. I can't realize it at all.
Mother and death seem so impossible, her life brimmed
over so.
Ever yours

Helen

Bronwen remembered Grandmamma Noble, small and trim,
who died three years before I was born.

Mother's two sisters—her favourite younger sister Mary
Geraldine, and her rather formidable elder one, Irene—had
both married. Uncle Lance, the youngest of the family, we
did not meet for many years. Aunt Mary had married a
handsome young consulting engineer, one of a big family of
jolly brothers and sisters; Uncle Arthur Valon was full of fun
and popular with his nephews and nieces. Their daughter
Margaret, born between Merfyn and Bronwen, was my
specially beloved cousin who often came to stay with us,
sometimes with her mother. Unlike Bronwen, she adored
little children and enjoyed playing with me, pushing me in
the small mail-cart and telling me stories.
    Aunt Irene had married Hugh McArthur, a delightful man.
He had two interesting maiden sisters, each of whom did
welfare work, one among the desperately poor cotton
operatives of Manchester. The McArthurs visited us less
frequently. Aunt Irene had no children of her own and
took no interest in us; moreover she disapproved of Edward's

and Helen's marriage. The McArthurs lived in a flat in Grosvenor Road which overlooked the Thames. They were tremendous cyclists, and they walked a great deal too. Uncle Hugh was tall and angular, with a long face and drooping moustache. He usually wore a Norfolk jacket and knickerbockers, and thick knitted stockings with fancy turnover tops, carefully re-heeled and darned by his wife. He was kind and gentle, but we were never very easy with Aunt Irene, who seemed stern and disapproving.

As children we travelled a good deal with one or both of our parents. I wish I could remember going by train with my father to visit Granny and Gappa Thomas in their tall, dark, basemented house in Balham, to Aunt Mary's at Duke's Avenue in Chiswick, or to the de la Mare family. Bronwen went to Wales several times with her father and vividly remembered the ferry at Laugharne, and the ferryman who carried passengers one by one on his back through the shallows to the shore. Edward's friend, Thomas Seccombe, went with them on one occasion. He was a very tall, large man, who had to have a bicycle specially built to carry his big frame. Bronwen never forgot his clambering on to the back of the ferryman, who was already carrying the enormous bicycle.

Like the rest of us, Bronwen was a little in awe of Gappa, and remembered especially being taken by him to a service at the Positivist Chapel off Lambs Conduit Street, Bloomsbury, and being patted on the head by large, bearded gentlemen in frock coats.

Gappa always wanted to know how we were getting on with our reading and school work. He would take us for long walks on Wandsworth Common, asking questions and talking hard. But as he was so tall one only caught a word here and there and was too nervous to keep saying 'What did you say?' so one answered yes or no indiscriminately, which didn't always fit what he was saying. He would walk

at his usual brisk pace, and grasped firmly by the hand we
would trot beside him, our short legs aching more and more.
However even with him Bronwen sometimes went her own
way. Once when he was staying with us at Berryfield he
asked Bronwen to walk to church with him. 'No,' she said,
'I'm going dunging.' And away she went down the lane,
carrying bucket and shovel for the droppings of the tradesmen's horses, so good for the garden.

Granny, on the other hand, was soft-voiced and gentle.
She wore long skirts with mysterious hidden pockets, and
always a wide, black, stuff belt into which was tucked her
little gold and blue-enamelled half-hunter watch on a long
gold chain. This watch was a source of delight and wonder
to me: Granny would slip it from her belt, hold it out, and
invite me to blow: magically the lid would fly open. When
she had time, Granny would roll Bronwen's or my hair into
tight papers before we went to bed. The unaccustomed
knobbiness of our heads was happily endured for the glory
of the curls when Granny unrolled the curl-papers in the
morning, brushing each lock round her finger. At the house
in Balham there was a fierce Welsh cook named Emma, who
lived most of the time in the basement and wore a very
long, white, starched apron.

I first met my father's five handsome brothers on their
occasional visits to Granny's house. Like their father, they
were tall and dark, whereas Edward, the eldest, was fair
and blue-eyed like his mother. They all had deep, soft,
attractive speaking voices. Uncle Ernest was the quietest of
the brothers. He was tall and loose-limbed with a swinging
walk which Mother always said was just like Edward's way
of walking. Ernest was an artist and earned his living by
designing posters and advertisements for an agency. In

those days this kind of work was seldom signed, but to us the pretty girls on his posters for the Underground were as recognizable as Barribal's fluffy young ladies. He spoke in a mocking way, seldom smiling, and when he was amused he looked slightly sardonic, with a sideways smile. Ernest had married Florrie Witts, a tall, rather angular but attractive cockney girl who had served in a tobacco shop. They had a son, Dick, to whom I was devoted. He was a little younger than I. Like his mother he had an eager vitality, and was always full of excitement and plans. For instance, when we went to the seaside he said he would throw off his clothes and jump off the last groyne—without even testing how cold it was. He knew, he said, exactly how to cope with a charging bull, too: one should just stand still until the animal was within a few feet and then calmly step aside so that the bull got his horns caught in the hedge—then one simply strolled away.

After the war I stayed occasionally with Auntie Florrie and Uncle Ernest in their small flat in Sheen. Uncle Ernest made a painting of me reading Dick's *Playbox Annual,* my spectacles crooked where I had knocked them.

Auntie Florrie had a sister, Venie, small, quiet, and palely pretty. She wore a high surgical boot and walked with a painful heavy movement, and played the piano in a cinema. Their father had been a tram-driver; widowed early, he had brought up the two girls himself, very strictly. Florrie, the headstrong tomboy, had once had his belt across her back; she had saved up weekly pennies to buy some silver bangles which she jingled on her wrist at the tea-table. 'Where did you get that rubbish?' he asked. 'Saved up and bought 'em,' said Florrie. 'Take them off,' ordered her father. At first Florrie pretended she couldn't get them off, but seeing the game was up, she slid them off her wrist. Her father took the bangles, twisted them into a silver knot and put them on the fire; then he gave her a cut with his belt and sent her to bed. Florrie was often sent to bed for being late, for tearing her clothes or for wearing out good boot-leather playing hop-scotch. Venie never married, but lived in a bed-sitting room with Tiddles, her large ginger and white cat, quietly dying of consumption.

Florrie was easily upset and inclined to nag at Dick and Uncle Ernest. I don't think she had much happiness with her silent, sardonic husband. He would often get up half-way through a meal and without a word take his cap and stick and swing out of the flat, leaving her warm-hearted cockney spirit frustrated. Her cockney lore fascinated us. For instance, she would say that if one ate a boiled egg without salt one would get worms; and speaking of a mean person: 'He threw his money about like a man with no arms.' Although he didn't have much to throw about I think perhaps Uncle Ernest was one of these; Florrie received only a very small share. She always carried her marriage lines tucked into the top of her corsets.

Uncle Ernest's portrait of Edward, dated 1905 and now in the National Portrait Gallery, is not, Mother always insisted, a good likeness.

I don't remember seeing Uncle Oscar at Granny's house; his connections with the theatre and a lady called Blanche Tomlin may possibly have kept him away from his stern father. Throughout their childhood the six boys had been discouraged from bringing their friends to the house. Oscar's work was to do with motor tyres. He was handsome and well-groomed, and had great charm. Later he often came to Otford for the weekend and was a kindly audience for my dancing. When we lived at Otford we were on a party telephone line, with five other subscribers—Sevenoaks 325Y4—and when the bell rang four times it was for us. Uncle Oscar would answer the telephone and putting on a comic voice would say, 'This is the sewage works—what's your trouble?' which I thought hilariously wicked. Bronwen was a great favourite of his and he often took her to the theatre; he had a passion for *Peter Pan* which he had seen thirty-four times. He drank a fair amount of whisky and was always genial and affectionate. His invariable farewell seemed to me as a little girl the most romantic in the world—'And may the roses blossom in your heart, 'til I come to gather them again.'

Uncle Dorie—short for Theodore—must have been Gappa's pride and joy. He too had worked his way up through the Civil Service, in public transport. He was married to Auntie Gertrude, a handsome, stately lady, and they lived in a large house at Forest Gate with their two boys, Ivor and Philip. Uncle Dorie played the piano well and would regularly practise for half an hour when he got back from the office in the evening. He lived an orderly life regulated by the clock. Ivor, tall and fair and extremely handsome, was two or three years older than I, and kind and gentle. I was frightened of his dark and stocky brother, Philip. In the garden he would tease me with worms, threatening to put them in my mouth.

In the 1930s Uncle Dorie was made Traffic Manager of the London Passenger Transport Board, and miraculously overnight on every bus and tram in London there appeared the words THEODORE EASTAWAY THOMAS—TRAFFIC MANAGER, painted in small white letters.

At that time one saw everywhere in London beautiful posters advertising the Underground, all designed by famous artists. One of these, by Richard Nevinson—son of H. W. Nevinson who had been such a friend to Edward at the beginning of his writing career—illustrated the poem 'Thaw':

> Over the land freckled with snow half-thawed
> The speculating rooks at their nests cawed

And saw from elm-tops, delicate as flower of grass,
What we below could not see, Winter pass.

These lines of Edward's were printed below an oil-painting
of treetops and rooks. Just before the Second World War I
wrote to Uncle Dorie and asked if it would be possible to
buy the original painting. I didn't hear from him immediately
and I felt I had been tactless and brash to ask. But soon the
picture, beautifully framed, arrived at my cottage door, a
wonderful present for me.

By this time Uncle Dorie had married again. Aunt Elsie
was homely and even-tempered, managing without fuss to
have Uncle's meals punctual to the minute, and fitting in
with his minutely-ordered time-table. In 1939 he was res-
ponsible for the transport arrangements made for the
evacuation of London children, and later received a knight-
hood. He spent a happy retirement at Eastbourne, going
for his constitutional along the front at precisely the same
time every day and returning punctually.

Uncle Reggie, dark and handsome, with curly hair, was
my favourite. He could play and sing at the piano, and like
Oscar was connected with the stage—concert parties and
music hall. I only saw him once or twice at Granny's house,
looking very fine in his uniform. I remember Auntie Madge
being mentioned now and again, but I don't know whether
she belonged to Oscar or Reggie. He learned map-reading
from his brother Edward at Hare Hall camp, but did not go
to France. My last memory of Uncle Reggie is of sitting beside him in the chilly, rather fusty, front room at Granny's
house, on a stool by the piano, its ornamental fretwork
backed with faded green silk, either side of which were
the moveable candle-holders. I remember being entranced
by his singing sentimental ballads, with tears in his eyes,
and being puzzled at the chorus of the one which ended,

'. . . across the faun', wondering what fauns had to do with
the ocean that separated Uncle Reggie from his sweetheart.
Long afterwards, I realized the word was 'foam'. Uncle
Reggie died in the influenza epidemic in 1919 before he was
demobilized.

Uncle Julian, the youngest of the brothers, all his life
devoted to Edward and his memory, was tall and delicate.
He and his wife Auntie Maud came to Granny's house more
frequently than any of the brothers, apart from Edward. I
remember them well because they brought their two little
children, Cicely, a toddler, and Edward, crawling. I adored
babies when I could nurse them on my lap. David and Elizabeth Ceinwen followed later.

Uncle Julian's four children and I are now all that remain
of that generation of the Thomas family.

Mary, mother's younger sister, with her prosperous, hard-
working husband lived in Chiswick and kept a living-in maid,
Amy Gunner. Their only child Margaret, whom I called
Margon, was gentle and quiet and had two long plaits:
the hair on the crown of her head was wavy, with little
curling tendrils over her ears and in the nape of her neck
between the plaits. Margon came to stay with us at Steep,
and our family stayed with hers in their comfortable spacious house, with a telephone and a gramophone—things I
had never seen before. Auntie Mary was firm, but very
warm-hearted and hospitable. As I was not yet at school I
was perhaps the niece they knew best, for if mother went to
stay at Chiswick, then I went with her.

Later on Bronwen was to live with them for a time when
with Margaret she attended Norland Place School and had
exercises for her round shoulders.

I looked forward to staying with Aunt Mary—it was only

there that I could bear to be separated from Mother—for we
went shopping in Chiswick High Road, sometimes riding on
trams where I collected the exotic purple, magenta and
emerald tram tickets, so much more exciting than the
wishy-washy coloured bus tickets. We always called in at a
dairy for cream cheese and I would be given a glass of milk
and cream, a great treat; Aunt Mary would say, 'Why, you've
got a white moustache,' and fish out of her pocket a clean
hankie smelling of Trefoil scent to wipe my mouth. The big
draper's shop was a special magical pleasure for it had a cash
railway. When the shop assistant screwed the bill and the
money into the little cylinder, put it on the wire with a neat
twist and pulled the brass handle, so that the cylinder
whizzed out of sight along the wire close to the ceiling—how
in the world did it return a moment later with exactly the
right change? Oh happy shop-lady, who measured yards of
ribbon with its underlining of white paper exactly the same
width as the ribbon, on the brass measure let into the
polished wood counter, and had charge of the cash railway.
Sometimes instead of a farthing change one was given a pink
paper neatly stuck with several rows of dressmaker's pins.

At Aunt Mary's house I was allowed to turn the handle of
the knife-cleaner—a tall object rather like a penny-in-the-
slot machine, with slots of different sizes for large and small
knives. I have no idea what happened inside this kind of
mangle, but the steel knives came out bright and shining. I
was allowed to stay in the kitchen and talk to Amy while
she washed up, and I sang sad songs to her, like 'Sweet
William'. I have never heard it since; it was one of the songs
my parents sang by the fire after my bath, and a special
favourite:

> O Father, Father, come build me a boat
> That on the ocean I may float

And every flagship I chance to meet
I will enquire for my William sweet—

    For a maid, a maid, I shall never be
    Till apples grow on an orange tree.

I had not gone more than half an hour
When I espied a man-o'-war
O Captain, Captain, come tell me true
Is my sweet William on board of you?

    For a maid . . .

O no fine lady, he is not here,
That he is drowned most breaks my fear
The other night when the wind blew high
'Twas then you lost your sweet sailor-boy

    For a maid . . .

I'll sit me down and I'll write a song
I'll write it neat and I'll write it long
At every line I will drop a tear
At ev'ry verse I'll set 'My Willie dear'

    For a maid, a maid, I shall never be
    Till apples grow on an orange tree.

I loved, too, 'Little Sir William', who was stabbed with his
school penknife on Easter Day and left to drown in the
Boyne Water; 'All round my hat I will wear a green willow',
and 'Where have you been all the day, Randal my son?'—
Randal who had eaten his sweetheart's proffered snake-pie.
Sometimes Amy read to me out of *Helen's Babies*, but I

really only wanted the same bit again and again—where the child wants the back of the watch opened to 'see the wheels go round'. Amy preferred the sad and pious *Jessica's First Prayer*, which was in penny novelette form, with paper covers and steel engravings of the unreformed Jessica covering with her bare foot the sixpence dropped by the whiskered, top-hatted gentleman.

Another treat at Chiswick was to be shown my Uncle Arthur's masonic regalia—royal blue satin studded with gleaming gems and enamelled emblems. In his satin apron and chain of office I imagined him looking like a splendid Red Indian brave. Much of the glamour went from these fantasies when I learned that the ornaments were worn over a dinner jacket. Still, there was always the delicious secrecy, for except for the legendary lady hiding in the grandfather clock, no woman would ever get a glimpse of Masonic ceremonies. But one day I might perhaps go with my uncle to the Ladies' Night banquet, when every guest found a costly present beside her plate—a feather fan, a silver powder compact, or even a tiny bedside clock from Aspreys. Each year Auntie Mary had a new evening dress made specially for Ladies' Night, of magenta, purple or royal blue satin, with milanese silk stockings and satin slippers dyed to match the dress.

It was soon after the outbreak of war in 1914 that the first gramophone I ever saw was played to me at my aunt's house as a great treat. The enchantment of imagining those tiny ladies and gentlemen singing and dancing inside the box! I would peer up through the wooden louvres when the two doors were opened and fancy I caught the swirl of a frilly petticoat or the glint of a white evening shirt-front. I did not, however, fancy the idea of a tiny German, dressed in grey uniform and coal-scuttle helmet—as in the newspaper cartoons—saying over and over again, 'Voz you dere? Voz you dere?' on a comic record called 'The German on the telephone'. Would he one day squeeze through the louvres and confront me? The picture of the plump white 'His Master's Voice' dog, head cocked, listening and looking down the big cone-shaped horn, whose portrait was on all the records, convinced me that he *saw* what was only just hidden from me—the tiny people on minute gilt chairs resting until required to dance 'Valse Triste'.

Still another joy at Chiswick was my uncle's pianola. Sometimes when he came home from his office in Victoria Street he would choose one of the many rolls of mysteriously patterned paper, fix it in a recess on the front of the piano between the two candle-holders, and pedal away to turn the cylinder; the keys would move as it played a Chopin Nocturne or Mazurka.

If I visited my aunt in term-time I might be lucky enough to be taken to Miss Bear's School of Deportment where my cousin Margaret was a pupil. The girls were dressed in azure-blue short skirts, with woollen stockings to match, white silk shirt blouses, blue ties and white gym shoes. I was told not to stare at Princess Mary, who was also a pupil, as she was shy and didn't like to be noticed. I thought her most beautiful, with neatly arranged flaxen curls held in place at the back of her head by a flat blue velvet bow. These elegant girls played ball to music, swung Swedish clubs in breath-taking patterns, 'And—one, two, swing', or walked round the hall with books on their heads or even a white ball. After each exercise, when the teacher, dressed like the girls in blue and white with a pretty diamond fob watch pinned to her busty blouse, called 'Rest!' the Princess would hurry to the chair beside her governess, who spread a lacey Shetland shawl over her shoulders until the next exercise.

Our relatives all lived in London then, and for our visits to them we wore 'best' clothes all the time!

A MONTH or so before my third birthday the family moved to a small cottage in Steep. Although it must have meant leaving some of the larger furniture at Wick Green, Mother enjoyed her first experience of living in a village. I can imagine her using to the full her great gift for arranging, and making the cottage cosy and pretty, and planting the garden with flowers. Edward, meanwhile, having taken cuttings from the Old Man plant (also called Lad's Love) which grew by the Bee House study and which Gordon Bottomley had first given him, and from other favourite plants, dug and cultivated the vegetable patch, chopped firewood and filled the coal-scuttle. When all was shipshape and Bristol fashion he would go up to his study and write. Later on Mother and I would go a little way to meet him returning, listening for his distant *coo-ee* and answering it until we could see him striding towards us.

Our neighbours in the pair of cottages were Mr and Mrs Dodd and their boy Tommy, who was about my age. If he got half a chance, Tommy would dive his grubby fist into the salt jar and stuff handfuls of salt into his mouth; for this he got a slap from his mother who warned him that his blood would dry up. In spite of my short sight, or perhaps because of it, I must have been observant, and also rather unnaturally fastidious. I remember our own and our neighbours' privies particularly. They were, of course, earth-closets. Ours was always fresh and wholesome, with a box of sifted earth which my father dealt with in the early morning. But next door to us ashes were used instead of earth, and these gave off a fusty, sour smell; instead of crepey paper in a roll, a copy of Bradshaw's railway time-table hung on a string. The paper was stiff and shiny, though it was fun tearing off the pages.

In the evenings, after tea, when we sat round the kitchen fire with Mother preparing to wash me in the zinc bath in front of the range, my father smoking his clay-pipe would perhaps need to clean one which had become brown and bitter. He would blow up the fire, put some sticks on and when they were glowing embers put the stained pipe right into the red glow, leave it awhile, then draw it out with the tongs, cool it on the hearth and it would again be as white as chalk. The sealing-wax tip he always put on would of course have melted away, so he would light a spill at the fire—Bronwen was a great spill-maker—take a stick of red sealing-wax and make a new mouth-piece on the renewed pipe. This was to avoid the clay sticking to the lips and perhaps pulling off the delicate skin.

Once he let Tommy and me play soap bubbles with two of his bigger clays. But Tommy got over-excited and ran down the path, stumbled, and the pipe-stem lodged in the roof of his mouth. Ever since then it has been imprinted on my memory and if I see a child running with anything in its mouth, I cannot help my fear; and I shrilly threaten the offender with Tommy's fate.

Another time Tommy and I had been bouncing in our muddy shoes on Mother's big bed with its white honeycomb counterpane, when my father appeared, picked us up, one under each arm, carried us downstairs and spanked us.

Merfyn and Bronwen now had a much shorter walk to Bedales; only five minutes instead of two miles or so. Edward was once questioning Merfyn about his school work and got the usual reply after the enquiry, 'What did you do today?' 'Oh, nothing much.' He persisted and said, 'Does Mr Scott take you out on Nature walks?' 'Sometimes.' 'What do you do on these walks?' 'Oh, nothing much.' 'But you must do something. Doesn't Mr Scott talk to you at all?' 'Yes, sometimes.' 'Doesn't he tell you about the plants, trees, birds and

so on that you see? What does he say?' 'Oh, he says "Keep
up, boys!" ' which made Edward laugh, as it so much
expressed not only the master's lack of interest in taking
reluctant small boys for a walk, but the boys' complete
boredom.

To help with the housekeeping, children from Bedales,
whose parents were abroad, sometimes spent the holidays with
us. Peter Mrosowsky was one of these. Up to the time he came
to Bedales he had spent most of his childhood in a Jesuit
monastery and knew nothing of family life. He was Merfyn's
age, dark, fierce and handsome. He and Merfyn fought now
and then and my father had to separate them. Peter was
travelling with us on the day war broke out in 1914, a nightmare journey which Mother never forgot. We were to join my
father at a farmhouse near to the Robert Frosts in Hereford-
shire. Years later, when we met Peter again as a prosperous
business man with several beautiful daughters, he always
remembered Mother's rock-cakes and our homely cottage
with affection. When she died, he stood in church, a tall,
handsome, elderly man, his cheeks wet with tears.

On winter days at Steep, when Mother was busy teaching
her foreign ladies, I spent many happy hours upstairs in the
chilly bedroom, dressing up a small ladder-back chair and
talking to it. Mother was occasionally given parcels of
scarcely worn girls' clothes by a well-to-do lady who lived
in the village. But alas on the whole they were far too grand
for me to wear or even for Mother to alter to more suitable
garments. It was these clothes perhaps that first gave me a
longing for lacey, flouncy frills, so unsuitable for my tall,
angular shape, which has never been outgrown—and neither
has the longing. But I delighted to hang a whole change of
clothes on the uprights of the chair—my elegant and biddable
playmate—chemise, liberty bodice, flannel petticoat, tucked
and herringboned, next the white cotton one frilled with

lace at hem and neck, and lastly the frothy party frock, all broderie anglaise frills, tied with its wide satin sash around the middle of the chairback. I was content to admire them hanging so gracefully on the shoulders of the chair and not to be wearing these fancy things myself.

We had plenty of visitors: apart from my cousin Margaret, who was best of all, Eleanor Farjeon was the one I looked forward to most. For Eleanor and I kept up a constant exchange of letters. I think Eleanor chose the names: she was Cocky Peacock and I was Polly Parrot. I always wished I had been the handsome peacock, with delicate crest like a princess's crown. Her letters were mostly in pictures, which I had to read myself, and mine were mostly written in my left-handed 'looking-glass writing' which Mother spelt out for me. Mother gave me daily lessons from an old-fashioned little blue book called *Reading without Tears*. I was learning to read fast, but I could not spell and write words yet. I remember Eleanor writing to tell me that she was bringing me a birthday present and I was to guess what it was; the drawing was of a box on rough wooden wheels, with a piece of string to pull it along. I was terribly disappointed that she should think such a babyish pull-cart was a suitable toy for me and I almost dreaded her coming. But when she did come it was a beautiful dolls' pram, which I took everywhere, except of course on long walks with my father, when I needed a free hand to hold his. Eleanor was full of fun, telling stories, singing and dancing. She could draw beautifully, too. I would describe the dress I wanted the princess in the story to wear and there she would be, appearing on paper from Eleanor's pencil.

Often Eleanor would walk over to Steep with her brothers, Bertie and Joe, and their friends. One summer day Mother was expecting them all. After spending a hot morning in the kitchen baking bread, scones, gingerbread and rock cakes, she laid tea in the cool sitting-room. I see it in my mind's eye: freshly baked goodies on plates covered with clean tea towels, a saucer of Mrs Dennet's deep yellow butter sprigged with parsley, a jar of homemade damson jam and another of Lupton's honey. The tea service was of white earthenware edged with a wreath of flowers and leaves in red, blue and green. The arrival of so many laughing ladies and gentlemen with walking sticks and rucksacks made me shy and silent. As we sat down to tea, while mother poured out I watched the sugar bowl and milk jug, suddenly noticing an unusual addition to the tea tray. There was a slight lull and I said, 'Aren't we swanky today; we've got a slop basin.' This made them all laugh, and I didn't dare look up again.

The poem my father wrote for me was so true! When I had learned to read it I was sorrowful for many years for I thought he could not have loved me: there were so many chinks in my armour—straight hair, spectacles and 'Wanting a thousand little things, that time without contentment brings'. There was always something I longed for and when it was mine, the expected happiness never quite followed. There was, for instance, the hat with cherries that I wanted so very much. 'They're not *real* cherries, you know.' 'Yes, I *know*.' I wheedled and made promises and at last the hat was bought. When the elastic under my chin—always too tight at first—had been loosened, I was entranced to hear and feel the red and purple cherries bobbing on the stiff straw brim. After admiring my reflection in shop windows, skipping along to make the cherries bounce, not looking where I was going and nearly bumping into people, there was a quiet time on my own when I had to be sure about those great glossy cherries. I could see that the leaves were not real but made of stiff waxy cloth. But the cherries themselves, such succulent perfection! I pressed my finger-nail through the skin of a red cherry; it split quite easily and out bulged its white cotton-wool stuffing. That one certainly wasn't the real thing, but this purple one, surely— and soon the cherries all round the hat lay disembowelled in a desolation of grubby cotton-wool and I sobbed inconsolably over my lost finery, which somehow I had expected would magically turn back to its former glossy glory.

On the other hand, I was a sharp, rather precocious child. My beloved Aunt Mary often reminded me of the time when the wind was taken completely out of her sails.

We had had a Russian lady staying with us, to whom Mother was giving English lessons. I had named a new kitten Teeka which, I declared, was Russian for 'dear little Pussy'. Auntie Mary came to visit us and when I showed her the kitten, she asked very knowingly what its name was.

'Teeka,' I replied. 'It's a Russian name.'

'Yes,' said my aunt proudly, 'and *I* know what it means.'

'Well, what then?' said I, crestfallen.

'It is Russian for "dear little Pussy".'

'Oh no it isn't. It means "just to make her look pretty",' I answered smugly.

My father must have been there at the time as he mentions Teeka in a letter to his friend John Freeman.

I had as a small girl an aversion to anything male, apart from my immediate family and friends. All my toys were called by girls' names and I would have nothing to do with a fluffy toy dog which had the name Toby on its collar.

On 16 November 1915, Edward wrote to Robert Frost:

Now I am going to trim a hedge and have tea with Bronwen while Helen fetches Baba from a dancing class. Baba said the other day 'The only thing I should like to be *in the way of men* is a Scottie with a kilt.' I asked what she

would like to be 'in the way of women' and she said
'*a widow*'.

I was proud of my father in his uniform and enjoyed
watching him polish the brass buttons on his tunic, using a
button-stick to keep the polish off the khaki. In May
1916 he wrote to Robert:

> As I was walking home with Helen and Baba last week,
> Baba asked whether Mrs ———'s baby was a boy or a girl?
> 'A boy.' 'Everyone has boys.' But, I said, boys were
> wanted to replace the dead. 'You don't think I haven't
> heard that before, my lad, do you?' she said to me. She
> is acquisitive and not generous, but she gets her own way
> without annoying much. I have some new songs for her
> from camp, and rather more for you.

I have recently been reading for the first time my father's
letters to Robert Frost. For most of my life I have felt that
he did not care for me. It gave me a deep shock of pleasure
to know that he reported my sayings and doings and that I
was just as dear and amusing to him as were Merfyn and
Bronwen. Apparently he frequently took me to London for
a week or so when he went to do some research in the
British Museum library. I remember well a time when he was
irritable with me. He had a cold bath every morning and I
had asked if I too could have one. I remember standing
shivering in the zinc bath and filling the sponge with cold
water and squeezing it against my chest while leaning forward so that no water touched me, and eventually being
yanked out and dried rather roughly, whimpering at my
cowardice. My sister's memories and adoration of her father
and his delight in the 'Merry one' helped to increase this
feeling of being the non-favourite.

I have happy memories too: the happiest were the walks
Edward and I took together and I have had a renewed

pleasure when reading his poems, which sometimes told of
these walks, in, for instance, 'The Cherry Trees'. I had seen
their scattered petals and remarked, 'Someone's been
married.'

> The cherry trees bend over and are shedding
> On the old road where all that passed are dead,
> Their petals, strewing the grass as for a wedding
> This early May morn when there is none to wed.

On 23 May 1915 Edward wrote to Frost: 'I hope you have a
dooryard as neat as ours is, with all the old man and rosemary
and lavender strong and the vegetable rows fairly continuous
and parallel and the may thick in the hedge.' He had already,
in December 1914, written the poem which Mother declared
was the one that most evoked his complex nature of self-
doubt, musing introspection and honesty. I am proud to
remember that I was the villain 'snipping the tips':

> Old Man, or Lad's-love—in the name there's nothing
> To one that knows not Lad's-love, or Old Man,
> The hoar-green feathery herb, almost a tree,
> Growing with rosemary and lavender.
> Even to one that knows it well, the names
> Half decorate, half perplex, the thing it is:
> At least, what that is clings not to the names
> In spite of time. And yet I like the names.
>
> The herb itself I like not, but for certain
> I love it, as some day the child will love it
> Who plucks a feather from the door-side bush
> Whenever she goes in or out of the house.
> Often she waits there, snipping the tips and shrivelling
> The shreds at last on to the path, perhaps
> Thinking, perhaps of nothing, till she sniffs
> Her fingers and runs off. The bush is still

But half as tall as she, though it is as old;
So well she clips it. Not a word she says;
And I can only wonder how much hereafter
She will remember, with that bitter scent
Of garden rows, and ancient damson-trees
Topping a hedge, a bent path to a door,
A low thick bush beside the door, and me
Forbidding her to pick.

                    As for myself,
Where first I met the bitter scent is lost.
I, too, often shrivel the grey shreds,
Sniff them and think and sniff again and try
Once more to think what it is I am remembering,
Always in vain. I cannot like the scent,
Yet I would rather give up others more sweet,
With no meaning, than this bitter one.

I have mislaid the key. I sniff the spray
And think of nothing; I see and I hear nothing;
Yet seem, too, to be listening, lying in wait
For what I should, yet never can, remember:
No garden appears, no path, no hoar-green bush
Of Lad's-love, or Old Man, no child beside,
Neither father, nor mother, nor any playmate;
Only an avenue, dark, nameless, without end.

That was the second of our Old Man cuttings: the first came
from Gordon Bottomley for the Wick Green garden, the
second was planted at Yew Tree Cottages. Since that time
we have always taken a cutting with us and planted it in
the next garden. A bush of Old Man flourishes on Edward's
grave at Agny, near Arras in France, and on Mother's grave
in Eastbury churchyard. When Lord David Cecil came to

Eastbury on the occasion of the dedication of Laurence Whistler's exquisite church window which celebrates the lives of Helen and Edward, he read this poem beautifully, and later drove home with a cutting of Lad's Love which he tells me flourishes still in his Dorset garden.

The walk with Edward that I remember most vividly is the setting for the poem called 'The Brook'. In the year 1973 Anne Mallinson of the Selborne Bookshop, and John Bowen, instituted the Edward Thomas Birthday Walk, and this takes place on the first Sunday in March. In 1979 the Walk set out from Bramdean Common, near Steep—the scene of 'The Brook'. I half wanted to join in to see if it was as I have remembered so clearly, but on the other hand feared I would not recognize it. In my mind's eye it is high summer and very still and I see the site as though I were a kestrel questing above it. Green slopes of short turf are either side of the stream, where my father sits reading and smoking his clay, perhaps writing in his notebook. Not far from where I am paddling in the swift shallow water is an arched stone bridge. There is a sharp pain in the soles of my bare feet, which look greenish in the stippled water. It is very still and serene as I scramble out of the stream and join my father; he rubs my feet, crinkled and cold. We sit there quietly and the silence is intense and I have that strange certainty and excitement that comes only once or twice in a lifetime, which I share—'No one's been here before.'

> Seated once by a brook, watching a child
> Chiefly that paddled, I was thus beguiled.
> Mellow the blackbird sang and sharp the thrush
> Not far off in the oak and hazel brush,
> Unseen. There was a scent like honeycomb

From mugwort dull. And down upon the dome
Of the stone the cart-horse kicks against so oft
A butterfly alighted. From aloft
He took the heat of the sun, and from below.
On the hot stone he perched contented so,
As if never a cart would pass again
That way; as if I were the last of men
And he the first of insects to have earth
And sun together and to know their worth.
I was divided between him and the gleam,
The motion, and the voices, of the stream,
The waters running frizzled over gravel,
That never vanish and for ever travel.
A grey flycatcher silent on a fence
And I sat as if we had been there since
The horseman and the horse lying beneath
The fir-tree-covered barrow on the heath,
The horseman and the horse with silver shoes,
Galloped the downs last. All that I could lose
I lost. And then the child's voice raised the dead.
'No one's been here before' was what she said
And what I felt, yet never should have found
A word for, while I gathered sight and sound.

How enviable was the crunching sound of my father's heavy
walking-shoes on the gritty lanes, as pleasing as the sound of
a horse munching hay. How delightful it would be, I thought,
when my insignificantly small feet, now making scarcely a
sound, would grow large and crunch as his did. 'There'll be a
wren's nest in that old wall, see, there's a cranny,' and we'd
stop and he would peer in and I'd peer in, but usually could
not see what he could see. Then his long gentle finger would
touch the eggs I could not reach.

In those two crowded years before my father went to
France, we stayed once or twice with Vivian and Dorothy
Locke-Ellis in their large and, to us, luxurious house in
Sussex. My father liked to work in a stone out-building in
their very large garden, and he recalls it in 'The Long Small
Room':

> The long small room that showed willows in the west
> Narrowed up to the end the fireplace filled,
> Although not wide. I liked it. No one guessed
> What need or accident made them so build.
>
> Only the moon, the mouse and the sparrow peeped
> In from the ivy round the casement thick.
> Of all they saw and heard there they shall keep
> The tale for the old ivy and older brick.
>
> When I look back I am like moon, sparrow and mouse
> That witnessed what they could never understand
> Or alter or prevent in the dark house.
> One thing remains the same—this my right hand
>
> Crawling crab-like over the clean white page,
> Resting awhile each morning on the pillow,
> Then once more starting to crawl on towards age.
> The hundred last leaves stream upon the willow.

Vivian had a motor which he drove unpredictably, once
bumping over the grass verge, to my terror, so that in sub-
sequent rides which were meant to be a great treat, I would
beg Dorothy to tell him not to 'go on the grass'. This and
watching him eat his breakfast porridge with a trickle of
cream running down his chin, which had been badly patched
up after a careless shave with a blob of cotton-wool, offended
my nervous and fastidious fussiness. Dorothy was beautiful

and delicate, and much admired by Bronwen for the elegant chiffon tea-gowns she sometimes wore in the afternoon, while lying on a cushioned chaise-longue in the drawing-room. She cured Bronwen of her nail-biting, by painting the stubby bits of finger-nail with her nail varnish, and then comparing the result with her own shapely fingers. I recall my first taste of creamy trifle flavoured with a dash of sherry; and the shame and pain of the doctor's having to lance a boil which prevented me from sitting down.

I remember walking with mother from Selsfield House to the post after a heavy rainstorm, when the road was scattered with elm flowers, red and squiggly, which I could not avoid treading on; I became paralysed with disgust thinking they were drowned red worms and would not move for screaming. Perhaps that was before I was fitted with spectacles and could not see well. Mother was irritated and impatient with me, promising they were not worms, but it was no good.

But a walk with my father from Selsfield was horrifying in an interesting way, for we came across a gamekeeper's vermin pole. But this was not a pole but the branch of a tree, hanging low, with his victims strung up to warn off marauding birds and animals from the pheasant chicks he was rearing. The dangling withered carcases of crows, weasels, jays, an owl and a scarcely recognisable cat, their fur or feathers faded by the rain to earth colour, eyeless and swaying clumsily, filled me with a gruesome fascination. 'Can they feel, do they mind being dead, was that a cat, someone's own cat, are they cold, why are they there, why are they dead?'

In July 1916 Edward wrote to Eleanor: 'At the Ellises I could not help writing these four verses on the theme of some stories I used to tell Baba there.' My pencilled copy of the poem has 'For Baba' at the top.

There was a weasel lived in the sun
With all his family,
Till a keeper shot him with his gun
And hung him up on a tree,
Where he swings in the wind and rain,
In the sun and in the snow,
Without pleasure, without pain,
On the dead oak tree bough.

There was a crow who was no sleeper,
But a thief and a murderer
Till a very late hour; and this keeper
Made him one of the things that were,
To hang and flap in rain and wind,
In the sun and in the snow.
There are no more sins to be sinned
On the dead oak tree bough.

There was a magpie, too,
Had a long tongue and a long tail;
He could both talk and do—
But what did that avail?
He, too, flaps in the wind and rain
Alongside weasel and crow,
Without pleasure, without pain,
On the dead oak tree bough.

And many other beasts
And birds, skin, bone and feather,
Have been taken from their feasts
And hung up there together,
To swing and have endless leisure
In the sun and in the snow,
Without pain, without pleasure,
On the dead oak tree bough.

Now in 1916, it was time to move from the cosiness of
Steep, for Merfyn was to be apprenticed to the drawing-
office of an engineering works at Walthamstow and my
father was to be posted to Hare Hall camp near Romford in
Essex as map instructor. Our new home had been a nurseryman's cottage right on the edge of Epping Forest, with no
near neighbours and no proper village. Edward wrote to
Robert Frost: 'We like our new home. Except on Saturday
and Sunday we see nothing only aeroplanes and deer in
the forest. Baba has no companions—she goes about telling
herself stories. She is a sensitive selfish little creature. Helen
has only her, so I suppose she must be spoilt. The others are
really only at home to sleep except at weekends.'

He wrote to Eleanor: 'I won't speak of the book to Baba.
But when I asked her what I had given her and promised her
6d if she remembered she said, on reflection, "A kiss", which
in fact is all I did give her; so she earned 6d.'

> What shall I give my daughter the younger
> More than will keep her from cold and hunger?
> I shall not give her anything.
> If she shared South Weald and Havering,
> Their acres, the two brooks running between,
> Paine's Brook and Weald Brook,
> With pewit, woodpecker, swan, and rook,
> She would be no richer than the queen
> Who once on a time sat in Havering Bower
> Alone, with the shadows, pleasure and power.
> She could do no more with Samarcand,
> Or the mountains of a mountain land
> And its far white house above cottages
> Like Venus above the Pleiades.
> Her small hands I would not cumber
> With so many acres and their lumber,

But leave her Steep and her own world
And her spectacled self with hair uncurled,
Wanting a thousand little things
That time without contentment brings.

THAT last Christmas for us as a complete family was spent in the Nurseryman's cottage on the edge of Epping Forest. The snow was deep and the forest trees heavily laden, and Daddy at the last moment was coming home on leave.

The house seemed bulging with secrets and I was forbidden to look in cupboards, boxes, even into Mother's work-basket. My father's sudden homecoming had filled the place with gaiety. It was no longer an effort for Mother to create that wonderful festive feeling which she loved to do. Until the arrival of Edward's telegram the preparations must have been heavy-hearted in spite of her determination that the children should have a happy Christmas. Now it was all different. The cake was iced, the turkey stuffed, the parcels sent by post hidden away, the cards put up on the mantelpiece, the forest searched for holly.

An almost unbearable suspense and excitement—should I *ever* get to sleep that Christmas Eve? Because if Father Christmas found me awake, there would be an empty stocking. Sleep must have come, for I awoke in the white darkness of the early morning and crept from the cosy warmth to the foot of the bed to feel the glorious bulging stocking hanging there, with a trumpet lolling over the top. Daddy was already downstairs, greatcoat over pyjamas, brewing tea; and when he carried up the tray of steaming cups, Bronwen, Merfyn and I all squeezed into their big bed to open our treasures. Stockings never had the proper presents in them, but exciting little oddments, all done up in crisp tissue paper, a painting book, crayons, bags of sweets, white sugar mice with pink eyes and string tails, a Russian lady of bright painted wood, containing a smaller and she a smaller still until there were five Russian ladies and one tiny Russian baby at the end. Merfyn's stocking had always, and continued to have in all the years that we

four spent Christmas together, a mouth organ. Besides the
mouth organ was an assortment of B D V cigarettes with
their beautiful silk 'cards', shaving soap, a comb for his
springy curls, which I so much envied and loved to brush,
and to see the curls spring back again. Bronwen's stocking
had delicious grown-up things like tiny bottles of scent,
emery boards for her nails, sketch pad and Venus pencils,
hair ribbons and lacey hankie.

This year Merfyn immediately played 'It's a long way
to Tipperary' and 'When Irish eyes are smiling'. I still
had a doll's tiny feeding bottle to unwrap, and a grey
clockwork mouse which Daddy wound up. Mother and we
girls obligingly screamed as it scurried over the floor. Second
cups of tea were brought and then we dressed hurriedly and
ate a quick breakfast, for there on chairs and stools were
our five piles of 'proper' presents in their brown paper or
Christmas wrappings. Mother had dressed me a doll, and
had made several outfits, including a schoolgirl's with gym
tunic, white blouse and tie. I hastily admired the tiny
trousseau, undid the buttons and fastenings, and dressed the
doll in an old baby dress of mine. Wrapping her up in a
grubby shawl, I tucked her up in the doll's bed which I
found inside another parcel.

In a huge parcel of presents beautifully wrapped in pretty
paper and with tinselled ribbon, Eleanor Farjeon had sent
Edward a large box of crystallized fruits, for he had an insa-
tiable sweet tooth; but alas, they all—pears, apricots, green-
gages and cherries—tasted strongly of varnish. Mother had
earlier received an unexpected cheque for £20 and had
bought Edward a beautiful Jaeger sleeping-bag, with double
top; Edward wrote in marking-ink, on the specially provided
tape, P. E. THOMAS. Bronwen crouched over the fire,
crunching nuts and reading *Girl of the Limberlost*.

While I was helping Mother to lay the tea in the kitchen,

with crackers by each plate, there was a sudden quiet in the little parlour and when it was time to call the others to tea, there was a Christmas tree, its coloured candles lit, and decorated with the most wonderful things I had ever seen: tinsel and spun glass ornaments glittering in the candle-light, and at the top a beautiful fairy, sparkling and smiling and waving her wand. What a Christmas! Never before had I seen a Christmas tree. Merfyn had dug it up from the forest some days before, and it had been carefully hidden in the wood-shed.

After I had been allowed to blow out the red, green and white stubs of the candles, and the lamp was lit in the sitting-room, the fire made up with wood collected from the forest, the family contentedly reading, crunching nuts or peeling oranges, I'm sure I would have remembered the wonderful proof Merfyn had had of Father Christmas's coming. He had hung up his stocking—it was always one of Mother's old, well-darned ones—in the chimney corner at Elses Farm, leaving an orange as a present: and in the morning, beside the bulging stocking was 'Thank you' in letters cut out in orange peel! Mother read me several poems from *The Golden Staircase*, the fat anthology given to me by my father; and then I sat on his knee while he sang my favourite Welsh song, 'Gweneth gwyn', and romping ones he had sung in camp and which were easy to learn. Now I stood on a chair by the window, the curtains not yet drawn, feeling the magic of Christmas, my father's large, strong hand on my shoulder, looking out into the white, still forest, straining with my short-sighted eyes behind the small spectacles, hoping to see perhaps the deer with antlered heads and pricked ears, and whispering 'Shall we see any?' Are they out there? Are they cold and frightened? I wish I could see some, or even just one.' The cosy lamplight, the rising flames of the fire, my father's hand: safe, warm and content. Perhaps he was already thinking of the poem he would write when he was back at camp, and send to me:

> Out in the dark over the snow
> The fallow fawns invisible go
> With the fallow doe;
> And the winds blow
> Fast as the stars are slow.
>
> Stealthily the dark haunts round
> And, when a lamp goes, without sound
> At a swifter bound
> Than the swiftest hound,
> Arrives, and all else is drowned;
>
> And I and star and wind and deer,
> Are in the dark together,—near,
> Yet far,—and fear
> Drums on my ear
> In that sage company drear.
>
> How weak and little is the light,
> All the universe of sight,
> Love and delight,
> Before the might,
> If you love it not, of night.

The first of the only two letters I ever had from my father must have reached me on the last day of 1916. It was posted on 30 December.

R. A. MESS
TINTOWN
LYDD

29.xii.16

My dear Myfanwy,

I am so glad you haven't got that nasty tooth any longer, and I hope you don't dislike the dentist who took it away. But you did enjoy your Christmas, didn't you? I know I did. I mean I enjoyed your Christmas and mine too. When I got here I found two more presents, a pocket writing case from Uncle Oscar and a piece of cake from Eleanor.

Did Mother tell you I wrote a poem about the dark that evening when you did not want to go into the sitting room because it was dark? Eleanor perhaps will type it and then I will send you a copy.

I am going to be very much alone for a few days, because the man who sleeps in my room is going home to Scotland. I think I shall like being alone.

On Monday and Wednesday we are going to shoot with real guns. I don't quite now what I shall have to do. (You see I have spelt 'know' without a k.) But as one of us is away the rest will be uncommonly busy from now onwards. I should not be surprised if we were in France at the end of this month. I do hope peace won't come just yet. I should not know what to do, especially if it came before I had really been a soldier. I wonder if you want peace, and if you can remember when there was no war.

It really is very solitary by this smoky fire with the wind rattling the door, shaking it and making the lock sound as if it were somebody trying to come in but finding the door locked and knowing there was somebody inside who *could* open it.

I think if I had a chair or a table I should write verses just for something to do before bedtime. Perhaps I will try.

Give Mother and Merfyn and Bronwen each a love for me and tell Mother her letter came this afternoon after I posted my second one to her.   Goodbye.

                                                        Daddy

Towards the end of January 1917 I stayed with Arthur
Ransome's wife, Ivy, and their daughter Tabitha, in their
farmhouse near Tisbury. Ivy was strikingly handsome in a
gipsy way, which was enhanced by her full skirts, high-
laced boots, 'peasant' blouses, hooped ear-rings and bright
beads, and most of all perhaps by her elaborately arranged
hair, with plaits and loops and ringlets, and a flat curve over
her forehead to hide an ugly scar. Tabitha was pale and
plump with two long snakey plaits. And like gipsies we
drove about in a donkey cart which took us over rough
tracks on the downs. Kitty Gurd was her maid-of-all-work.
Ivy's mother was staying there too. Arthur Ransome was in
Russia. Years after I learned that he was said to have skated
over the frozen Volga with Lenin's daughter. Constantly Ivy
would sing to the rather languid Tabitha:

> What is the matter with Tabitha R?
>   She's ALL RIGHT.
> What is the matter with Tabitha R?
>   SHE'S all right.
> Now her Daddy is far away
> Then her Mummy has time to play
> What is the matter with Tabitha R?
>   SHE'S ALL RIGHT!

The tune is very clear in my mind still. Ivy read aloud to us
The Fairchild Family, a moral story in which the naughty
child is burned to death.

One evening Tabitha and I were bouncing on a wide couch
and I put out my leg and tripped her over so that she fell, but
on the couch. I was in disgrace for this and terrified by all the
things Ivy and Kitty Gurd told me might have happened to
Tabitha's back had she not fallen on the soft couch. I was
put to bed and in my snivelling loneliness could hear the old
song drifting up to me from the cosy sitting-room.

Ivy's prim mother said to me one day, 'I'm sure your father sings beautiful folk songs to you, can you remember any to sing to me?' Always willing to show off I rejoiced her with 'Gor blimey O'Riley you *are* looking well' and 'Cover up anything red, sir, cover up anything red, sir, cover up anything red, sir, So I covered up me old Dad's nose'—two of the latest songs from camp which Daddy had sung to us round the fire at Christmas. These were received with tight-lipped disapproval and I was not asked to sing again.

My father, who had had his embarkation leave and was waiting for orders to sail, wrote in his diary on 27 January 1917:

A clear windy frosty dawn, the sun like a bright coin between the knuckles of opposite hills seen from sidelong. A fox. A little office work. Telegram to say Baba was at Ransome's, so I walked over Downs by Chicklade Bottom and the Fonthills to Hatch, and blistered both feet badly. House full of ice and big fires. Sat up with Ivy till 12 and slept till 8. Another fine bright frosty day on the 28th. Wrote to Bronwen, Helen, Ivy, Eleanor. Letters from Bronwen, Helen, Mother, Eleanor. Slept late. Rested my feet, talking to the children or Ivy cooking with Kitty Gurd. Hired a bicycle to save walking. Such a beautiful ride after joining the Mere and Amesbury Road at Font-hill Bishop—hedgeless roads over long sloping downs with woods and sprinkled thorns, carved with old tracks which junipers line—an owl and many rabbits—a clear pale sky and but a faint sunset—a long twilight lasting till 6. We are to move at 6.30 a.m. tomorrow. Horton and Smith and I dined together laughing at imbecile jests and at Smith's own laughing. . . .

At Ivy's house, I sat on his knee in the chimney corner of the big sitting-room, he smoking his clay and singing to me,

gently amused to hear about the 'folk songs' I had sung to
Ivy's mother. I awoke in the night, safe and content in the
crook of his arm. We said goodbye the next morning, and
watched him out of sight on the bicycle he had borrowed.
He sailed on the 29th, crossing to Le Havre at night.

After saying goodbye to my father, every night for weeks
I prayed for his safety on the ship, which seemed to me the
only dangerous part of going to war. I imagined huge waves
dashing against a small tug-boat, which mounted to the crest
and then slithered down. My eyes screwed up tightly
could not dispel this terrifying picture. The only other
prayer I knew was one which Joan Farjeon, Joe's daughter,
had taught me. This prayer was a puzzle but I did not like
to ask Mother about it: we were not a praying family. But
seeing Joan kneel by her bed enchanted me and I became a
regular kneeler. The prayer I learned from her was:

> Gentle Jesus meek and mild
> Look upon a little child
> Pity mice and plicity
> Suffer me to come to Thee
> Four corners to my bed
> Four angels round my head
> One to watch and one to pray
> And two to bear my soul away.

To pity mice seemed logical and proper, disliked and
trapped as they were, but what in the world was *plicity*? I
came across the prayer many years later and felt a great fool
to have pitied mice. A friend had the same puzzlement over
the hymn 'Can a mother's tender care cease towards the
child she bear? ' Why were he-bears excluded?

The time came for me to go back to High Beech. The dangers
of the sea were over now, and I had no further fear. One

saw funny pictures by Heath Robinson of soldiers at the Front, and occasionally we saw overhead white bursts of anti-aircraft fire. But Mother's terror and anxiety for my father's safety were carefully hidden so as not to distress us. She was making me an emerald green coat with a set of small brass Artists' Rifle buttons down the front. We walked up to the post every day, which I dreaded as we had to pass the school playground which bordered the road. The boys would shout 'Hullo four-eyes' or 'Gig-lamps, there goes gig-lamps'. I could tell by the jeering tone of their voices that it was something unpleasant, but I had to ask Mother what it meant. How I hated my offending spectacles!

The second and last letter I had from my father came from France with the FIELD POST OFFICE postmark dated 24 March 1917 and overstamped with the oval red mark saying PASSED FIELD CENSOR—4227.

The letter is written in pencil on paper torn from a notebook and has two sketches.

My dear Baba,

One day I saw a house or a big barn in the country where the Germans were, with a little roof over a pump or a well alongside of it, like this: [sketch].

But next morning when I looked all I could see was the little roof like this: [sketch].

All the trees were gone and the house was gone. Also the Germans have gone and since then I have been right up there and seen Cockneys and Scotchmen but no Germans. It is a funny country. Now I expect the French people will be coming up to that village to see if there are any walls left of their houses and anything in their gardens.

Now you have come back to your house and found all the bricks there and perhaps some new things in the garden. You are going to have Joy, too, aren't you? I wish I could see you in the forest. There is no forest here and no copses even very near, and no hedges at all, so that there are not so many birds, but plenty of chaffinches and larks, no peacocks, no swans. There are lots of little children about as old as you are, but without specs, living in the cottages here.

Now I hear I have to get up early and do a hard day's work tomorrow, so I must go to bed.

Goodnight, Nos da y chwi.   Daddy

Sometimes I would walk to the corner on my own to sit on a log and wait for Bronwen walking back from school at Loughton. I was joined on one occasion by a very respectably dressed man, who began to chat to me. To forestall any offering of sweets which I felt might be an embarrassment to both of us I quickly ventured the information that my father was a policeman, and felt quite safe. The man walked off after that and I felt I was in control.

But on that bright April day after Easter, when mother was sewing and I was awkwardly filling in the pricked dots on a postcard with coloured wool, embroidering a wild duck to send to France, I saw the telegraph boy lean his red bicycle against the fence. Mother stood reading the message with a face of stone. 'No answer' came like a croak, and the boy rode away. Mother fetched our coats and we went shivering out into the sunny April afternoon. I clutched her hand, half-running to keep up with her quick firm step, glancing continually up at the graven face that did not turn to meet my look. There were no children in the playground as we hurried to the post office, no calls which I could not have borne—for although I knew the shouts of 'Four Eyes' were aimed at me, Mother also wore spectacles. I waited, with dry mouth and chilled heart, outside the post office, while wires were sent off to Mother's sisters, to Granny and to Eleanor.

The day after, before arrangements were made for us to go to London to stay with Auntie Mary, I was looking at my favourite picture in a story book, an engraving which Bron had delicately coloured for me. Suddenly I ripped it out, screwed it up and flung it on the fire in a rage of tears—for what couldn't possibly happen to us had happened. My father would never come back. Why had I only prayed for his safety crossing the stormy sea? No answer.

FROM the time of the telegram, recollections of High Beech are few. Probably I was not there much, but staying with the John Freemans at Anerley, with Eleanor in her country cottage, or with Granny or Auntie Mary, while Mother was looking for a house she could afford to rent, in Kent where she and Edward had been happy. I don't think she ever went back to Steep again, except to stay with Lord Horder at the foot of the Shoulder of Mutton—but that was long, long afterwards. I remember Edward Garnett's coming to see mother at High Beech and his telling me rather sharply to go and play, which wounded me; I had a shock of fear that he would separate me from Mother. That was the only time I saw him, tall, large and bushy-browed. Ever since, whenever I have heard his name I have been reminded of the hurt of being impatiently dismissed, without a caress.

Staying with the Freemans, air-raids were exciting adventures. Directly the maroon sounded I was carried downstairs wrapped in an eiderdown, as were the Freeman children, Cathy and Joy, and we were given mugs of sweet cocoa and cake until the raid was over. And once I heard the strange sound of, as it seemed, all London clapping and cheering as a Zeppelin was brought down in flames.

It was during one of these stays with the Freemans that I had my first taste of school at the kindergarten Cathy and Joy attended, where we played singing games and there was a dancing class on the lawn. I was entranced by the grace of a child named Joan Snow, who was often asked to dance alone to show the rest of us how a step should be done. I was ravished by her skilful movements and my love of dancing began then. (I have no recollection of the dancing class I evidently went to at Steep, which is mentioned in my father's letter.) Unless Mother was with me I was not happy

at the Freemans, being frightened by the unpredictable Cathy. She showed me a bunch of cigarette cards one day and asked me if I would like a 'pitcher'. I didn't connect this word with the cards and said 'No' hastily, as it probably meant would I like a pinch or a tweak of my hair. There were some dusty pullets in a pen at the bottom of their garden. We attempted to dress them in old baby clothes, but the moist sickly smell of the poor creatures disgusted me and I could not join in. They were given rides in the doll's pram, but we all reeked of the sweaty smell.

Staying with Granny now was gloomy, and she spoke little to me, though Gappa would embarrass me by asking questions about my memories of my father, a subject which was never spoken of at home or with my aunts and uncles. And poor Granny was hurt when I turned away from her soft, moist kisses. In those days children were expected to kiss and be kissed by anyone who came to the house; but I resented any kisses but Mother's.

Quite soon after my father's death, some neighbours of Auntie Mary in Duke's Avenue had a Canadian soldier on leave from France staying with them. He said he had been at Vimy Ridge and remembered my father—how everyone loved him, and how he had been smoking his pipe round the camp fire in the evening after a battle when he was killed. My mother had long talks with him and was greatly comforted to meet someone who was actually there, and who remembered Edward. We only learned years later that this soldier could not have known my father as Canadian regiments were nowhere near Arras at the time.

Edward's young commanding officer, Franklyn Lushington, told us that he was killed at the start of the battle of Arras, at about 7.30 in the morning of Easter Monday, 9th April, at his observation post in an old chalk quarry, his body untouched, his heart stopped by the vacuum of an unexploded shell. We have his watch, which stopped with his heart, and his pocket diary with its curious shell-like convolutions, a photograph of Helen inside.

But the idea of Edward's being killed at Vimy Ridge, as recounted by the Canadian soldier, became an accepted fact in our family and circle of friends, and it is perpetuated in Robert Frost's poem to Edward:

> I slumbered with your poems on my breast
> Spread open as I dropped them, half-read through
> Like dove wings on a figure on a tomb
> To see, if in the dream they brought of you,
>
> I might not have the chance I missed in life
> Through some delay, and call you to your face
> First soldier, and then poet, and then both,
> Who died a soldier-poet of your race.
>
> I meant, you meant, that nothing should remain
> Unsaid between us, brother, and this remained—
> And one thing more that was not then to say:
> The Victory for what it lost and gained.
>
> You went to meet the shell's embrace of fire
> On Vimy Ridge; and when you fell that day
> The war seemed over more for you than me,
> But now for me than you—the other way.
>
> How over, though, for even me who knew
> The foe thrust back unsafe beyond the Rhine,
> If I was not to speak of it to you
> And see you pleased once more with words of mine?

(There is nothing like typing a poem rather slowly to taste its quality—and perhaps to find it a poor thing.) But this one of Frost's, 'Iris by Night', has tenderness and magic:

> One misty evening, one another's guide,
> We two were groping down a Malvern side
> The last wet fields and dripping hedges home.
> There came a moment of confusing lights,
> Such as according to belief in Rome
> Were seen of old at Memphis on the heights
> Before the fragments of a former sun
> Could concentrate anew and rise as one.
> Light was a paste of pigment in our eyes.
> And there was a moon and then a scene
> So watery as to seem submarine;
> In which we two stood saturated, drowned.
> The clover-mingled rowan on the ground
> Had taken all the water it could as dew,
> And still the air was saturated too,
> Its airy pressure turned to water weight.
> Then a small rainbow like a trellis gate,
> A very small moon-made prismatic bow,
> Stood closely over us through which to go.
> And then we were vouchsafed the miracle
> That never yet to other two befell
> And I alone of us have lived to tell.
> A wonder! Bow and rainbow as it bent,
> Instead of moving with us as we went
> (To keep the pots of gold from being found),
> It lifted from its dewy pediment
> Its two mote-swimming many coloured ends
> And gathered them together in a ring.
> And we stood in it softly circled round
> From all division time or foe can bring
> In a relation of elected friends.

Staying with Eleanor at her country cottage at Billingshurst I was not desperately homesick away from Mother, but in other people's houses I had many times cried myself to a nightmare sleep. During my stay with Eleanor she was dearer than ever and it was the first time I had had her to myself or indeed been the guest of a grown-up where there were no other children. Moreover, she did not try to talk to me about Edward. She told wonderful stories, and drew and painted pictures to illustrate them, singing songs and playing tunes 'out of her head' as we used to say. She was already composing the enchanting 'Songs of London Town' and sang several of them to me—my favourites were always the poignant ones, 'St Mary Axe', 'St John lived in a wood, where elm-trees spread their branches', and 'I sat on the mill-wall, looking at the water'.

Eleanor knew that I had had a horror of snakes, ever since I had come across one in a hayfield, mortally wounded by the cutter yet still with its broken head, thrashing itself into coils one way then another; I was unable to move or to look away. 'It won't die until the sun goes down,' I was told, and it haunted my nights whenever I was restless or miserable. On a bright sunny morning Eleanor suggested a walk across a common; today's story was to be about a princess to whom everyone was unkind except a little blue and yellow snake, who lived curled up on the ledge of a warm rock. As we walked, there was a huge boulder by the path and in a cranny a beautifully jointed, brightly painted, wooden snake lay magically ready for me. All along our way objects which came into the story were there for me to find, partly hidden—a bead necklace, an apple, a pencil and notebook and other pretty fairings, together with a trim small basket to carry them in. Glorious magic! There was something very special about Eleanor. I loved watching her play the piano, or drawing, with those long fingers which turned back at

the tips. I have never again seen any like them. In later years
we saw Eleanor only occasionally, but she always gave us a
wonderful welcome, her arms spread wide for an enveloping
hug to which even Merfyn was happy to submit. She made
you feel, as some actors do, that you were the one person in
the world she most wanted to see. In her company you felt
in top form, sparkling, beautiful, elegant and witty. In the
years of childhood, we were—as I have said—Polly Parrot and
Cocky Peacock and I was good, and content to be with her.

Mother had now heard of a Tudor cottage, half a large house
in fact, in Otford, a village lying on the Pilgrims' Way, with
the ruined Palace of Wolsey and Thomas Becket close by. It
was owned by Canon and Mrs Gilchrist Thompson. She had
liked Mother's application to rent it and invited her to stay
for a few days at their house in Sevenoaks; I went too. This
was my first experience of a leisured and cultured family,
living in spacious and conventional comfort, with several
maids and menservants. After breakfast there were family
prayers in the large dining-room. First the maidservants,
then the boot-boy and the coachman-gardener came in and
stood in a little group near the door. At the long table we
stood behind our chairs, the Canon reading the Collect for
the Day, a short piece from the Bible, the Lord's Prayer, in
which we all joined, and then the blessing. This was followed
by the mistress of the house telling the parlourmaid she
could clear away the breakfast.

Bronwen had by this time gone back to Bedales, where
she had many friends, so that Mother and I were on our
own at High Beech for the move. The removal van was late
and the men were not only drunk, but rough and coarse in
behaviour and speech, straddling the ditch by the house
when relieving themselves. When the van finally reached

Otford, the precious books were tipped on to the floor of the living-room, and boxes of china—which luckily Mother had carefully packed herself—dumped anywhere, with furniture piled on top.

But home-making was Mother's great gift and her favourite undertaking, and in a day or two the sewing-machine was whirring and with a mouthful of pins the curtains were measured, hemmed and put up, chipped furniture polished —my father's own pieces of carpentry undamaged, so sturdily were they made—rugs beaten and laid, and all signs of the nightmarish move obliterated. We laughed at the low doorways, the latchet fastenings, the tiny doorway to my bedroom which even I had to stoop to get into, we black-leaded the grates, banged nails into walls for our pictures, and enjoyed the luxury of a proper bathroom for the first time for many years. The china was washed and placed on the dresser and mantelpiece, the geyser in the bathroom was inspected, the kitchen table scrubbed and, recharged with many cups of tea and hunks of bread and dripping, the cottage was soon ship-shape and Bristol fashion. There was gaslight in all the downstairs rooms, candles for upstairs, or oil-lamps if you liked to read in bed.

The living-room, into which the front door opened, had a huge open fireplace, wide enough to sit one each side behind the mantelpiece, with small ledges for holding a beer mug and hooks for smoking hams. The great beam across the hearth, forming the mantelshelf, was of chestnut, black and many years older than the cottage, with initials and a Star of David cut in the wood when it was workable, but now it was like iron, so that no nail could be hammered in to hold toasting fork or kettle holder. The sitting-room next door was a beautiful, large room, also with an open hearth—but this room we were soon to discover could only be used in warm weather because the fire smoked appallingly unless the outside door—a sort of second front door—were left open. Probably at one time the house was too large for the blacksmith and his family and had been divided into three, not two, as now in 1917. In front of the house, to separate it from the village street, was a row of stout posts threaded with loops of chain. There was a narrow flower border between the house and the posts, which Mother soon planted with bulbs, wallflowers and forget-me-nots and a grape vine which flourished and in a few years yielded tiny bunches of light red grapes about the size of currants. The memory of their taste still sets my teeth on edge!

Behind the cottage was a large unkempt garden which Mother enjoyed planning and making with lawns, flower beds, fruit trees and bushes and a vegetable plot, and an open summer house, four posts holding up a roof.

Across the road from our front steps was the post office and grocer's kept by the Warren family and known as Top Warrens, to differentiate them from a shop lower down the gentle slope to the river Darenth, which sold sweets, tobacco, minerals and newspapers, called Bottom Warrens. Both families were rather plump and pale, unsmiling to young customers, and it was to Bottom Warrens I went for my Sunday treat of cherry cider in a bottle with an imprisoned glass marble in its neck, and for my weekly comics, *The Rainbow* and *Wonderland*. Mr Bottom Warren had died long since and his brother lived with the family, well-groomed, with a slightly sinister stiff hand in an immaculate kid glove. I never discovered whether this was, as I hoped, a wooden hand, or just a paralysed one. But whichever it was, with the other he could make rich birthday, Christmas and wedding cakes, and ice them with gossamer patterns of flowers, butterflies and trellis-work. He had been a professional confectioner in London and in that rather doughy family had an unmistakable stylishness about him.

A little further down from Top Warrens was The Bull, the largest pub in the village, and nearby the village school, its playground bordering the road. Standing on the high window-ledges inside the school's narrow, streaky windows were jars containing snakes pickled in methylated spirit, the liquid cloudy and grey with disintegrating scales from the limp inmates. These windows had to be hurried past with turned head and a shudder. Mr Hoff, the schoolmaster, in stained black suit and soiled celluloid collar, for me personified Mr Squeers, while many of the boys in the playground could have been Poor Smike. Their roughness frightened me and I dreaded lest they should call out 'Four eyes'.

Near the school was The Old Parsonage, a beautiful house with wrought-iron gates and a pigeon-loft running from end to end of the pitched roof which dated from the time when Otford was an important ecclesiastical centre and messages were sent to Canterbury by carrier pigeon. In this house, with its spacious gardens, lived the actor, Alan Anderson, and his wife and daughter, always known as John.

Still further on, after a row of terraced workmen's cottages, was an old timber and brick house called Pickmoss. Like our house, its windows had diamond-shaped panes, and a great nail-studded front door opened on to the street. Soon I was to have lessons there with Gabrielle Seagrim, whose father was a captain in France. Opposite Pickmoss, by the bridge over the Darenth, was the pub called The Horns, kept by Mr Lintott; beyond the bridge was the big house where the Underwoods lived. Mr Underwood was in the cinema business and drove to the station in an open carriage each morning in silk hat, cigar and large dahlia in his buttonhole. The Vicarage stood among some overgrown laurels and conifers this side of the bridge, dark and sunless.

If you turned left from our front steps, there was a lane going up to Park House, where lived Mrs Simmons, her

daughter Dorothy, who drove about in a smart dog-cart
drawn by a high-stepping chestnut mare, and her son Leslie,
who over twenty years later was to be Bronwen's third
husband. Also up this lane, but before you got to the big
house, was Mr Lowrie's workshop—he was a cabinet-maker
and Mrs Lowrie kept a small sweet-shop then, later to become a much larger grocery and hardware store. You
walked up the road, passed cottages with the front doors
opening on to the village street and a small pub called The
Crown, and there the road widened into the village green
with a large pond, the road encircling it. Surrounding the
pond with its stone banks were stone posts and rounded
iron bars on which one could hang upside down and turn
somersaults. Mr Knight and his sons Vic and Tom ran the
Village Stores opposite, the shop-windows an interesting
still-life of pie-dishes, oil-cans and funnels, yellowing pads of
writing paper, little dishes of rice, lentils and barley, fly-
papers, locust beans, jars of peardrops and bulls-eyes and
sticks of cough-candy, a pair of hob-nailed boots, and coils
of licorice bootlaces. Cough-candy was my favourite, but I
was not allowed it, as Grandmama Noble had told *her* children that paregoric contained a *drug*. Mother discouraged
me from the licorice bootlaces too—for her Mama knew that
it was made of ox's blood, in the same mysterious way in
which she knew the Italian ice-cream men kept the ice-
cream under their beds. Locust beans were repulsive to look
at, dried up dark brown crinkled pods, rather ear-shaped—
but they were 24 a penny and tempting at the price. The
first one eaten was very sweet, a little like the flavour of
dates, but hard and dry to chew; and by the third the sweet-
ness was cloying and the rest of the rich pennyworth was
hidden and forgotten.

Round the pond and set back from the village green were
fine Queen Anne and Georgian houses—the Macleans and

the Wellbands lived there. The church, with its squat spire, stood back from the village green. At the corner of the road to Sevenoaks lived Charlie Browning, the milkman. Leaving the pond on the right, if you kept to Mr Knight's side of the road you passed the fourth pub, The Woodman, at the corner of Leonard's Avenue. A bomb had fallen near the two terraces of sad-looking houses in this treeless avenue. Opposite Ilott's farm was the pretty cottage where Harvey, the Macleans' lady gardener lived, smart in breeches, tussore silk shirt, and close-cropped hair. Up the hill past the railway station were the Hunt kennels, with the Master living close by. At the top the road turned left to Shoreham and Eynsford, or right to the Pilgrims' Way and a mysterious house called Beechy Leas, which had a great copper dome on top.

Further down the village from the forge was Mr Groves, the butcher. A splendid bole of a beech-tree, its roots well below the sawdusted floor-boards, served as a chopping-block and was kept scrubbed and white. Mr Groves must surely have been the model for Mr Bones the Butcher in the game of 'Happy Families', side-whiskers, rosy cheeks and all. He wore the conventional straw boater, and blue and white-striped apron over a white starched coat; a steel hung from a leather strap slung round his waist.

The baker called every day, with a huge cane basket of warm, sweet-smelling loaves covered with a white tea-cloth, and the milkman with his gallon can on which were hung the shining measures with their polished brass hooked handles—the enchanting little gill measure for cream!

The fishmonger with his van—all the tradesmen had horse-drawn vehicles—often accompanied by lumbering fat bluebottles and an unpleasant smell, was fascinating to watch filleting a plaice or sole, with his red hands, covered with glinting fish-scales, so skilfully handling the broad-bladed knife, slicing off each side of the flat-fish so close to the backbone that no flesh was left on. Mother would never buy mackerel: she had lived at Southport where they were sold fresh from the sea—and once you had tasted these, she said, the much-travelled fish were slack and unpalatable.

Watching such simple but deftly practised skills delighted me: a butcher sharpening a knife or slicing steak; the quick turn of the wrist when Mr Hartnup, the blacksmith, twisted off the surplus point of a nail when shoeing a horse; a farm-worker in shirt-sleeves and braces, his cord trousers tied with string below the knee, with leisurely grace sharpening his scythe on a whetstone; a grocer weighing out tea and making the trim little oblong parcel, sweeping the few escaped leaves with a cupped hand into the open end and then folding it deftly in, patting the parcel into shape and tying it with string from a roll hung from the ceiling; butter being cut from the large yellow slab with the smooth, tapered butter-pat, then turned and shaped into an oblong on the marble slab after weighing on the scales and finally ridged across the top with the edge of the squat pat. Sugar too was weighed and poured from the lipped brass scoop into a cone-shaped poke made from the bright blue paper used only for sugar, so neat and secure yet without any fastening or string. Shopping was full of interest in those days; now there are hardly any polished wood counters left, and fewer skills are needed to serve customers.

Old Mr Knight, with his pointed beard and stubby fingers stained brown with tobacco was good to watch, too, his sharp clasp-knife slicing a half-ounce of Turk's Head tobacco from a shiny black coil into the polished brass balance.

In those early days at Otford, before I had anyone to play with, my chief pleasure was to watch Mr Hartnup working in his forge, shoeing the great plough-horses standing so patiently, the sweet, acrid smell of the hot shoe held against the pared hoof for fitting, and the soft sound of the seven tapered, four-sided nails being tapped through the shoe into the hoof. I would stay on, at a polite distance, while Mr Hartnup had his dinner outside the forge, sitting on his jacket on the rim of the wheelwright's circle, his leather apron a table cloth. First he would get his clasp-knife from his pocket, then he would undo the red and white spotted handkerchief, knotted at the corners, and spread it out beside him. Inside were the crusty top off a cottage loaf, a chunk of cheese and a peeled raw onion. He would begin by cutting a thick slice from the bread, a wedge of cheese and a sliver of onion, place the cheese and onion on the bread, cut off a good hunk with the clasp-knife and with the savoury pile still on the blade, put it into his mouth, hardly touching the food with his iron-stained hands. I marvelled how he managed not to take a slice off his tongue with the sharp blade, which was what I was told would happen if I ate with my knife. An obliging robin tidied up when Mr Hartnup shook out the spotted handkerchief, which was folded and put into his jacket pocket. Then out would come his pipe and tobacco tin. The pipe would be carefully packed, the tobacco first rolled in his palm, then lit with a hot coal from the forge and smoked in the doorway until the arrival of the next customer. And I would skip off home, arriving in time to scrape out the mixing bowl while Mother put a cake in the oven.

PLAYMATES AND NEIGHBOURS

AT Otford the first child I got to know was Kitty Fordham. In the school holidays she came with her mother who helped with the housework. It was understood that Mrs Fordham wouldn't do the laundry; that was considered a lower type of work and only done by the farm-workers' wives who were glad to make a shilling or two by taking in washing. Mr Fordham worked on the railway. You could always spot the railwaymen because with their dinner bags slung over their shoulders, they carried a neat little blue-enamel tea-can; turned the other way up the lid became a cup with a proper handle.

On Monday mornings before school a small boy would appear with a truck made from an orange box and old pram wheels, pulled by rope. The household washing in a sheet with a great knot of the four corners tied together, and safety-pinned on to this, a list of contents, would be trundled back home where mum or gran had the copper going well. In a day or two back would come the wicker washing-basket, the linen shining white, beautifully ironed and folded, tablecloths starched. When unpacked and the list checked, Mother would hang the laundry to air on a clothes-horse in front of the living-room fire where it would emit a warm fresh smell from its adventures in the copper, the mangle, the garden clothes-line, and an ironing blanket on the kitchen table, irons standing on the hob by the bars of the kitchen range. Mother was a great airer. She said it was asking for trouble if sheets or underclothes were not properly aired. I liked to see her press a folded garment to her lip and cheek to feel if it was still damp, in a pretty affectionate movement. All the processes of washing were interesting, especially the squeezing of the sheets after rinsing and before mangling; the sheet would be twisted and wrung out by the washerwoman's strong wrists, the wrung-out part twisting magically up her bare arm like a wrinkled snake.

At first Kitty Fordham was very shy and spoke little to me, nodding or shaking her head; but my dolls and their clothes soon altered her mother's 'Lost y'r tongue, our Kitty?' Kitty was surprised to hear I didn't go to school, as I was seven, though I had learned to read long since.

Kitty lived in Leonard's Avenue; after the bomb in 1916 it had a rather dishevelled appearance and a poor reputation. I sometimes went to tea with Kitty and so got to know other village girls who would come in after tea, Belle Kemp, Di Stears, the two Topsys, Queenie and Vi, and Dolly with the wooden leg, a stout, leather-covered, tapered piece of wood strapped to her thigh and waist. Her face was pale and had a waxy glisten, and a strange sweetish smell came from the warm leather casing of her leg. I often took to Kitty's house my most treasured possession, *The Golden Staircase*— the anthology of children's poetry my father had given me that last Christmas. We took it in turns to read the poems I chose: 'The Spider and the Fly', 'The Imps in the Heavenly Meadow', 'Young Lochinvar' and 'The Wreck of the Hesperus'. The book still has an initial pencilled beside some of the poems, so that I know who read them in that cosy kitchen, with rag rugs on the floor, the fly-catcher which hung from the ceiling, winter and summer—a sphere of coloured paper with intricate honeycomb patterns into which flies were supposed to wander and get lost. I thought it very handsome, but had a horror of the paper ball being jogged and all its dead lost flies shaking down on to the tea-table.

Occasionally one or two girls would come to tea with us at Forge House, and I was fascinated by their politeness: when asked if they took sugar in their tea, or when offered cake or biscuit, their toneless reply was 'I don't mind'. I pondered on this a great deal because one *did* mind very much—especially about taking sugar in tea. I couldn't possibly have drunk tea with sugar in it. Years later, soon after my daughter was born the Sister at Queen Charlotte's Hospital said to me briskly, 'Would you like a nice cup of tea, Mother?' 'Oh yes *please*,' I said. But when it came it was weak, tepid and sickeningly sweet. I couldn't drink it and burst into tears. But to these strictly brought up children perhaps to say 'Yes please' would seem too eager.

After school, on fine afternoons or on Saturdays, the girls played hopscotch in the village street, making big numbered squares on the road, scrawled with lumps of chalk from the garden, and we hopped, pushing a small piece of brick—stones wore out the toe-caps of boots, and mum would give them a 'clip side the ear-'ole' or chase them with the copper-stick. Most of the girls wore boots; some were buttoned up the sides, necessitating the use of a button-hook, some laced up the front almost to the knee. I hankered after a pair of boy's boots because they had blakeys in the soles which struck sparks from the flinty road, and the last four or five lacings were hooked round little studs, then the laces were wound round the tops and tied. Boys' bootlaces were made of leather.

The girls usually wore hats or tammies. They all had long hair, while mine was cut short with a fringe. Many of them had their hair very tightly plaited all the week, in twenty or more skinny plaits with the end turned up and tied with bits of rag. These pigtails would spin and flap when we played hopscotch or skipping. Two would turn the rope, stretched halfway across the village street, and first of all we took turns at running through without skipping, then we would jump—once, twice, and so on—to see who could keep in the longest. One trip and you were out. The initial running through without skipping needed accurate timing, for if one's feet got caught in the turning rope one fell sprawling on to the rough street and made a hole in the knee of a stocking. This too would incur a 'clip side the ear-'ole', or 'Mum will grumble at me'. As I wore short socks, grazed knees and hands were my penalty.

The boys played tops and hoops too, but never with the girls. The boys' tops were the mushroom-shaped window-breakers and their whips had leather bootlaces instead of string. Their tops leaped high in the air and when they fell would go on spinning and could be whipped up again. The girls' tops were stocky and pear-shaped and spun sedately on the ground; their hoops were wooden, some big enough to run through like a circus lady, or to skip with. They were bowled along with taps from a stick. Mr Hartnup made the boys' hoops from rounded iron and instead of wooden hoop-sticks they bowled theirs with iron hooks which stayed in contact with the hoop all the way, striking sparks and making a pleasant sound.

On the few occasions I had played with children of my own age before living in a village, I had learned to say 'Pax' which usually meant you had a stitch playing 'He' and 'Touch Wood' and could stop running without being 'had'. The Otford girls said 'Fainites' which I could not bring myself to say: though this was very like 'Fains I' which I later learned at school. If you said 'Fains I' quickly enough when you were asked to fetch something, you were exempted. The opposite of 'Bags I', in fact.

I learned from the Otford children two counting-out rhymes:

Eeny meeny miny mo
Catch a nigger by his toe
If he hollers let him go

Eeeny meeny miny mo
O U T spells out
And out you must GO!

Each peach
Pear
Plum
Out goes Number ONE!

But these were frowned on at the school I went to later in Sevenoaks. It was considered 'common' to use the word 'holler'. There I learned to hold out my two clenched fists while the leader said:

One potato, two potato,
Three potato, four,
Five potato, six potato,
Seven potato—MORE

and the owner of the fist touched as 'MORE' was 'he'.

From the Otford girls I learned a rollicking jingle with a catchy tune, which I believed was a Romany song. I practised it interminably at home until I could sing it faster than Vi, Belle, Di or Kitty:

Kyla merry kewty kyrie
Kyla merry kymo
Strim strim stram-a-diddle
Lanner panner rag-tag
Rignum bommanerry kylo.

Mother disapproved of 'Oo-er', an expression I'd learnt from Joy Freeman's cousin Lois. I noticed the Otford girls said it too. The most fearful threat from one of them was 'I'll tell my mum of you and she'll holler'. I had this shouted at me only once, and for the next two days I was afraid to go out to play, expecting to see Mrs Booker bearing down on me hollering and with a copper-stick in her fist.

In summer the girls played hopscotch, and ball games to rhymes like

> One two three allairy
> I see Sister Mary
> Sitting on a wool-allairy
> Kissing Tommy Atkins

or (last line) 'Eating choc'late babies', bouncing the ball, turning round and catching it, cocking a leg over it, throwing it up and clapping, once, twice, up to twenty times, on the same throw.

The girls never spoke to the boys, not even to their brothers. Some, like Queenie or Glad, would bring their young brothers or sisters in a push-chair and stand by, content to watch the others playing, proud to be minding the little 'n. I was always a willing nursemaid, and loved having a real baby to push, though very often the sight of my spectacled face would cause a baby to pucker up its face and yowl. In those days one rarely saw a child in specs. Often the boys' heads were shorn to the scalp, with bald white patches where they had ring-worm, a burrowing parasite caught from cows' hides, probably when giving dad a hand with the milking. Girls wouldn't have been welcome in the cow-shed, so they didn't get this unpleasant complaint; though I had been firmly told I was on no account to put on someone else's hat, to borrow, or lend, a comb. Mother told me later that when the gentry heard I played with village girls their immediate reaction was 'But they have *things* in their hair'. Dolly, with the peg-leg, would sit on her doorstep just above Mrs Lowrie's sweetshop and watch us playing, sometimes heaving herself up and offering kindly to turn one end of the rope.

Mother had several callers who left cards. She would repay the call, leaving her card, and staying the first time the requisite seventeen minutes. But the gentry in the big houses couldn't 'place' her: as a war widow she did not wear mourning, for Edward had hated the idea of parading grief by wearing dismal colours. So she had continued to wear her favourite rust colour and green and orange. There was a young war widow in the village who wore the conventional widow's weeds, a long flowing veil instead of a hat, her clothes entirely black; her little daughter had a black band round her coat-sleeve, which I envied. The fact that I played in the street with the village girls, and did not go to school, puzzled the ladies of the village; Mother sitting sewing on the front door-step and passing the time of day with who-ever went by, disconcerted them and once the formal duty calls were made they felt they had done enough to welcome a stranger.

The sad young widow in black lived with her in-laws in a pretty little house down by the Darenth. At Christmas a card came from her, asking me to a children's party, at the foot of which was printed 'Carriages at 6 p.m.' Not having mixed with other children, except outdoors, skipping or bowling hoops, I was shy and solemn at parties and had to be pushed by my hostess into 'joining in'. The part I liked best was at the end when 'Sir Roger de Coverley' was danced. I never had for a partner one of the few boys who came to parties. They were snatched by the smiling, pretty little girls. My partner was usually another plain girl, also reluctant to join in. But there was always a delicious moment when one ran forward, curtseyed to one of the boys and was whirled round by him to the sound of the intoxicating tune.

Early in 1918 Merfyn joined up in a Kentish regiment and came home on leave occasionally. For a time he was billetted in Wakefield Prison; he told us about the condemned cell, which was much more comfortable than the others. Bronwen was back at Bedales and often spent the holidays with school friends or at Auntie Mary's. She had grown into a beautiful girl, with high cheek-bones, wide brown eyes and delicate features, very like a photograph of Granny Thomas as a girl. Mother and I were very much on our own and I was painfully possessive and dependent upon her. If she visited a friend after I had been put to bed I couldn't sleep until I heard her quick firm step coming up the village street and had called out goodnight to her as she came in, just to let her know I was not asleep.

While waiting for the weekly bus to Sevenoaks one got to know those in the village who did not make formal calls or leave cards. We would gather in a scattered crowd of eight or so by the pond, chatting about the price of groceries or the weather. I was asked where I went to school, and noticed with anguish the look of disapproval when Mother said she had not decided about this yet and held my hand more tightly. My anguish was for Mother, for I felt reproach in their voices. With Merfyn and Bronwen away she was very much alone, and there was always the fear that Merfyn might be sent to France.

Nancy Richardson, a lively, unconventional young woman who lived with her elderly father in a charming cottage at the end of the village, near the river, was someone Mother got to know while waiting for the bus. Nancy was a keen gardener; her great friend was Harvey, the lady-gardener at the big house. Later on her brother's wife, Phyllis, with three small children, would come and stay with her. A life-long and happy friendship grew between our two families. On the whole, though, Mother had to depend on her friends coming for weekends, or on going to London for the day and visiting her sisters or Granny.

Although I had been to the theatre to see *Peter Pan* I had never been to church, so I persuaded Mother to take me to the children's service on Sunday afternoon. I felt in some way that church and the theatre were rather alike in that they both set out to please, and I persuaded myself that a children's service would have life-sized angels flying gracefully round the church on those invisible wires. I imagined their feathery wings and floating white draperies and the glint of their golden trumpets and harps. So that it was with a high heart and eager expectation that I was taken to church. Although I hadn't told Mother what I hoped for, she had done her best to tell me that it might not be very interesting and that I mustn't expect too much. Some of my hopes had come perhaps from my favourite game as a small child, when my parents would give me a 'flying angel'—holding on to my hands and running till I suddenly rose off the ground with a lovely catch of the breath. So with these happy thoughts of seeing perhaps Vi, Kitty and Topsy landing like thistledown on the rafters of the church, we pushed open the heavy door in which were embedded, roughly in the shape of a human body, the heads of nails which were said to have fastened the skin of an evil-doer who had been flayed alive. In the dark church Mrs Gidney, the piano teacher, was trying out hymn tunes, not on the organ but on a rather tinny piano. Scattered about the church were a dozen or so children, some with their mothers. 'When will there be angels?' I whispered to Mother, after I had peered into the roof for signs of wires. But before she had time to answer the service began, taken by the aloof and unsmiling vicar who intoned the prayers and read us a story. We sang 'There's a home' and 'All things bright and beautiful' including, of course, the verse about the rich man in his castle, the poor man at his gate, which is nowadays omitted. Then we shuffled out. The only bright spot was being given a card by the piano lady, with a picture of a real angel on the stamp, to show I had been to church.

I felt bitterly let down. But still hopeful, and enjoying having my card stamped with a different angel each week— one with gold on it for Easter—I attended regularly by my-self for some weeks. There was very little variation in the service, though one Sunday Vi came to church wearing her mother's false teeth which she had found in a mug in the kitchen while her parents had gone upstairs for the Sunday afternoon lie-down, and that made an interesting diversion.

I soon learned from Belle and Ivy that things were much better at the chapel below Bottom Warrens. There they had concerts, a treat in the Underwoods' garden, and prizes too. So I became a regular attender at the Wesleyan Chapel, which was full of women, children and a few old men, and where Miss Violet Underwood played rousing hymns on the harmonium, and lovely lilting ones like 'By coo-ool Silo-o-oam's sha-ady ri-ills'.

There were of course no games in the village street on Sundays. Not many boys were seen about, but the girls, with their week-old plaits undone and brushed out into a crimpy frizz, ornamented with floppy ribbon bows, walked down to Chapel in their white, starched and goffered pina-fores, with frills of broderie anglaise at neck, arm-holes and hem, over Sunday dresses, below which showed a little of the frilled white drawers and petticoats, unwrinkled black stockings and shiny Sunday boots. After Chapel, while Mum got the dinner on, some went for walks down the village, conscious of their fluffy hair and pretty frills, or perhaps up the side lanes to pick wildflowers. I went with them some-times and was interested that the girls spat when we passed a dead rabbit by the hedge: 'Mum says you must spit or

you'll get an illness.' I was repelled by the spitting, and
noticed that girls seemed unable to spit neatly, whereas the
boys, who frequently spat in imitation of their fathers,
could do it expertly, without any dribble. The girls weren't
supposed to run on Sunday or to call out after their friends.
They were usually sent off on a walk after Sunday dinner
had been cleared and washed up, when Mum and Dad went
upstairs for a 'lay-down' till tea-time.

On Sundays the village grandmothers wore black bonnets
resembling those worn by the old Queen Victoria. The bonnets rose above the forehead and were decorated in a way
that reminded me of the domed white plaster flowers in the
churchyard. But on the bonnets everything was black—
butterflies, ears of wheat, roses, lace, curled ostrich feathers,
glinting bugles, sprays of leaves and even bunches of cherries
—all were set about with ruched black ribbon and tied beneath the chin with a big black bow. I had a good view in
Chapel of these interesting confections.

My faith was strong, if rather theatrical, for on the many
occasions when I played by myself, the village children
being at school, I spent happy times hanging upside-down
on the smooth bars round the pond, my eyes tight shut,
willing Jesus to send down some young angels to play with
me—like those in one of my favourite poems, 'The Imps in
the Heavenly Meadow'—who would leave polishing their
haloes and flutter down, invisible to anyone but myself
and would perhaps teach me to fly. Hanging by my knees
with my head nearly touching the grass, with my uninter-
rupted view of the sky, I was in a good position to see the
clouds parting. I never lost hope or felt disappointed.

The first funeral I ever saw, slowly passing Forge House,
was watched with deep interest and admiration. The glass-
sided hearse was drawn by two black horses. Nodding black
ostrich plumes on their heads, their backs covered with

black palls edged with silver braid and long black silk
tassels, seemed fitting splendour for whoever lay under a
mass of wreaths and crosses. The hearse was followed by
several closed carriages, the black blinds drawn down.

Once I joined the girls by the churchyard wall to watch a
coffin being lowered into the grave; and later when all had
been made tidy and the mourners gone, we looked at the
flowers and read the messages on the black-edged cards.
Better, though, than the stiffly wired flowers of the wreaths,
were the immortal domed offerings to the quiet dead, the
icing-sugar roses, clasped hands, ribbons and doves with
olive branches and even butterflies, pristine and glistening
under their glass covers. It was perhaps the glass dome that I
admired and coveted most, for in some houses I had seen a
clock under a glass dome, a sumptuous arrangement of wax
flowers, grasses, waxen fruit, even a bird's nest and eggs,
made far more beautiful because of their inaccessibility. To
me they seemed beyond price.

Mother was shocked and distressed when she heard of my
hanging about the churchyard after the funeral, and I could
see she was near to tears at what she felt was unseemly. I
promised, also in tears, never to do it again. I did not know
why it had hurt her, but to have hurt her was enough to
make me miserable. She didn't mind my running widder-
shins round one of the listing stone tombs, and putting my
ear to one of the cracks fearfully hoping to hear the devil
speak. Neither did she seem to mind my joining the children
to run after Darkie Day's low cart, jangling with kettles to
be mended, piled up with faggots of pea-sticks, with the
leaky paraffin drum, cans and funnels on the back. He
would be crouched in the driver's seat, a greasy felt hat
pulled down over his long dark hair, matching his tangly
beard, whip idly in his hand, reins loosely held as his rough
pony clopped up the street. The boys called out 'Darkie

darkie Day' and tried to get a ride by clinging on to the oily tailboard, while the others, too scared to ride, called out 'Whip behind!' Darkie Day paid no attention, but any movement of the arm with the whip was enough to send the boys running in the opposite direction, while we girls giggled and whispered, 'Isn't he *awful*'.

The water-cart was much more fun, with its jets of water coming through a row of holes pierced in the metal cylinder which had been filled with a dipper from the Darenth. The boys would run under the arch of water jets trying not to get wetted; the man leading the horse as the dusty road was sweetened would flick his whip at the boys in a leisurely way.

Later on I realised I must be content with my own company most of the time. When I went in to Sevenoaks to do the shopping for Mother and when the list was worked through and the basket filled, I walked down to the open-air skating-rink—a rough and ready affair—where the entrance fee of sixpence included the hire of a pair of roller-skates and there was no time limit. I learned to skate by watching others, and then spent a happy hour launching myself round and round the asphalt, squatting on my heels, or just sailing and experiencing delicious sensations of skimming through the air. Then collecting my shopping basket I'd catch the bus back to Otford in time for dinner.

SUMMER HOLIDAYS

DURING the last summer of the war we took lodgings in a row of fishermen's cottages at a small village on the south coast near Seaford. It was a long time since I had seen the sea. The first time was at Hayling Island when I was about three years old, then at Bacton, and in 1914 or 1915, when the whole family stayed at Flansham, near Bognor, with James Guthrie, his wife, and their three boys, John, Robin and Totch. I fell in love with John; he was kind to me and I watched him floating on the waves and knew how glorious that must feel.

Old Mrs Farjeon (always known to us as Aunt Maggie), her eldest son Harry, and Joe Farjeon's daughter Joan, who was about my age, were staying near Seaford in the cottage next door to ours.

The guns on the other side of the Channel boomed and thudded most of the time. I felt no fear of them, only a strange kind of relief that they couldn't hurt my father any more. Aunt Maggie was a keen dipper-in-the-sea. She dressed for bathing in a magnificent two-piece outfit: a full-skirted, short-sleeved, knee-length, sailor-collared serge tunic over voluminous bloomers gathered below the knee into a white band, on her head one of the universal bathing caps of those days. It was made of orangey-pink rubber pleated into a tight band of reinforced rubber, with ample space in the top for any amount of long hair. The cap almost invariably rose up the forehead and looked like a bishop's mitre. If it didn't ride up, the tightness of the reinforced forehead piece gave one such a headache that it had to be pushed up anyway. The game old lady bobbed about in the shallows, the ample folds of her belted tunic ballooning out as she crouched waist-deep in the water.

I had met Harry Farjeon occasionally at the Farjeons' house in Fellows Road, Hampstead. A strange and unique person, he taught at the Royal Academy of Music or spent the day working in his room. He could not bear strong light, and curtains or blinds darkened any room he was in. He wore constantly a green eye-shade pulled down low on his forehead below his waving dark hair. Under that beaklike shade one imagined a pair of large brown eyes, like a hawk's —but I think I only caught a glimpse of his eyes once and they were moist, red-rimmed and heavy-lidded; I preferred the imagined eyes. Apart from his thick, rather long hair, everything else about him was small, narrow and birdlike. Aunt Maggie, who bought all his clothes for him, enjoyed recalling a time when she was buying shirts; the size of the collar was so small that the assistant said it would help if madam told him the age of her little boy. She replied, 'I don't think it would help, as my son is in his forties.' Harry Farjeon wore dark suits, buttoned high up the neck, with high, stiff collars. People's hands and voices have always influenced my likes and dislikes: his hands were long, slender and delicate, with fingers turning up at the tips like Eleanor's. His voice was rather high and like most of the Farjeons he rolled his 'r's' like a Frenchman. I adored him. He had a way with children, never talking down to them; and like his sister he could tell the most wonderful stories as Joan and I walked on either side of him along the paths above the sea. Out for a walk he wore a very large tweed peaked cap over his eyeshade. He looked down always, not at those he was speaking to. I don't remember Harry ever coming down to the beach with us, possibly the glint of sun on water would hurt his eyes; but Joan and I went for long walks with him, and I longed for him to take my hand in his. One day we passed the poster of a circus that was coming to Seaford during our holiday, and stopping to read

all the entrancing items, I said longingly how I should love
to see them. Harry told us how terribly the animals suffered,
the small dirty cages they were kept in, the cruel training
for undignified and stupid tricks, with whip and pointed
goad ever ready; how animals were terrified of fire and how
wicked it was to make horses jump through burning paper-
covered hoops. Joan and I were both in tears and I ran back
to the circus poster and ripped it down, making a solemn
vow never to go to a circus. I broke this vow about twenty-
five years later, very guiltily, when I took my daughter
Rosemary to see one. To my relief there were no lions and
no horses jumping through fire.

Joan called her uncle by the pet-name 'Harrativ', which I
thought unbecoming to this beloved, solemn and kindly
Prince of Elves. One Christmas he gave me a pendant with
an iridescent blue butterfly's wing imprisoned under glass.
I wore it for his sake and treasured it but I do remember
thinking it odd after his impassioned denunciation of circus
animals being exploited for our enjoyment.

We must have gone to the same place the following year. In
my mind's eye it is just a row of six fishermen's cottages at
right-angles to a road running high above the shingle beach,
ribbed with great tall breakwaters. I remember, not Aunt
Maggie and Joan on the beach this time, but my Mother and
me, my cousin Dick with his mother Auntie Florrie. Uncle
Ernest came down to see us once or twice on his motorbike.
I can remember Dick all the way in the train saying that the
moment he got to the beach he would put on his swimming
costume (as it was called then) and climb to the highest
breakwater and dive off. This entertained us all, but when it
came to the point, there was a thin, knobbly-kneed little
boy whimpering on the edge, hugging his chest, the outsize

bathing dress hanging in soggy wrinkles where the waves had splashed him, and afterwards sitting on the very edge of the retreating foam. There was an iron ladder down to a lower beach overhung by cliffs which was at first terrifying to climb. In the cliff face, very near this ladder, had been carved the profile of a Red Indian, a chief in his eagle feathers, about four feet high and deeply incised in the smooth rock. Uncle Ernest said it had been copied from an American silver dollar. Dick and I admired this carving immensely and were tremulous when we imagined the carver working away at such a dizzy height.

There was a terrible morning, which must have put an end to our visits to this lonely fishing village and shelving shingle beach. Mother and I, Auntie Florrie and Dick went to bathe before breakfast. We had changed up at the cottage and run down to the shore wrapped in our bathing towels. The tide was high and there were bouncing waves, so that Dick and I played in the spray at the edge, lying down to let the shingly stinging water just come up to our shoulders and feeling the pull of the pebbles beneath us as the waves sucked back again. We watched our mothers bobbing together, not far out but with just their heads and shoulders showing. It did not seem odd to me that Mother always kept her glasses on when in the sea, because I did too, otherwise we couldn't see what was happening on the sands, and got lost coming out of the sea after a swim. Dick and I were standing now, watching them bobbing together, and suddenly we clutched each other, for the faces of our mothers were strained and tense and sometimes the waves went over their heads. And they were much farther out. They could not get back and were clinging on to each other. The terrible feeling one has in dreams of not being able to make a sound came over us both. We pointed and tried to call out to them to come back to us. A man in white flannels

was cycling along the road and I tried to call out to him;
but he was already getting off his bicycle and was jumping
down the high sea wall on to the shingle and into the water.
We saw Mother hauled out between the man and Auntie
Florrie. She huddled on the shingle by the water's edge,
while Dick and I stood frozen stiff, shivering, watching her
dash off her spectacles to shatter on the pebbles. Bathing
towels were wrapped round her and the man helped her
up to the cottage, where she was put to bed with hot drinks,
stone hot-water-bottles and extra blankets. I have never
known such terror, though once Mother was rescued I knew
everything would be all right, she would not leave me.

THE WAR IS OVER

ONE dank November day the maroons sounded. White-faced, Mother said 'The war is over!' hugging me uncomfortably tight. I was disappointed that she and I did not go to the Mount to join the jollifications round the bonfire. We sat at home that dark chill evening, with Mother very quiet and unapproachable. I began to realize that many fathers, brothers, sons and sweethearts would now be coming home again. While the war was still on, we were suspended and always hopeful that a terrible mistake had been made and that my father would come home again. There had been many such mistakes. But now there was no more hope. Once when Mother was in London for the day she thought she caught a glimpse of Edward and ran after him. He got on to a bus and with a panting heart Mother took a taxi to follow it; the soldier got off at Victoria Station, with my Mother hurrying after him. He turned and she saw his face; faint and sick she stumbled to a bench—she had been wildly certain it was Edward.

Merfyn was safe and would later be demobilized. Soon it would be time for me to go to school.

My lessons with Gabrielle at Pickmoss were not very stimulating and I was frightened by the rows that went on between Gabrielle, Mrs Seagrim and the old lady who was the housekeeper. And when handsome Captain Seagrim came home on leave from France and I developed scabies, neither the lessons nor my visits to Pickmoss were continued once the long treatment for the burrowing parasites brought from the trenches was over. I was given baths in sulphur and daubed at night with yellow foggy-smelling ointment in quart-sized tins. I had to stay indoors, for poor Mother was far more ashamed of my having caught this disgusting complaint than if I had got things in my head from the village children.

It was arranged that I should cycle each day with the
vicar's daughter to the large girls' school in Sevenoaks. I
felt quite safe with Dorothy who was older than I—fourteen
or fifteen perhaps. On the first day she kindly left me in the
juniors' cloakroom and showed me a peg on which to hang
my coat and shoe bag.

I was utterly bewildered by the noise, the bustle, the
chatter. Somehow I found myself in a class-room and at a
desk, into which I put my fancy three-decker pencil box and
ruler. All I can recall of that first day was a feeling of shame
and inadequacy. 'Does anyone know a piece of poetry by
heart?' said the mistress, when we had settled down. 'Don't
call out, just hold up your hand.' Eager to please, my hand
shot up. 'Will you say your piece then, Miffawny?'

> The friendly cow all red and white,
> I love with all my heart:
> She gives me cream with all her might,
> To eat with apple-tart . . .

I began confidently.

'She wanders . . . She wanders . . .'. I gazed round, numbed,
some of the class had their hands over their mouths, sup-
pressing giggles. Some looked at me contemptuously: I had
not yet learned about 'showing-off'. The word 'lowing'
rather than 'mooing' had always pulled me up, but now
evaded me completely. My cheeks burned; the silence was
oppressive.

'You'd better sit down, then,' said the mistress, frowning
at this cocky new girl who should be taken down a peg.

Two other incidents stand out in the misery of that term.
I was fair game for teasing, being unused to children other
than the village girls who were kind and sought my friendship.
Every evening I was distracted by not being able to find my
coat or the shoe-bag on which Mother had embroidered my

initials in bright wools; they had invariably been put on a different peg. Every evening I feared an ambush of pinching, tweaking fingers, and I was terrified that Dorothy would cycle home without me. But she would come into the now empty cloakroom and help me find my belongings.

The one happy event was glorious and never experienced again: fire drill. This involved sliding down a great green tube of canvas from an upper window of the school and landing breathless on the grass. The other incident was my first experience and realization of corruption. I and another lonely child had found a dead frog, which we buried with ceremony and a prayer or two. About a fortnight later, hoping to find a beautiful white skeleton, I dug up the frog and found sludgy remains whose smell constricted my throat, filling my mouth with water, though I managed not to be sick. The vision of the decomposing frog and its stench kept me awake many nights and I was aware for the first time of this horrifying truth which must not only apply to frogs, dogs and cats, but to anything or anyone who was dead. I was haunted and prayed to be able to forget the frog. I didn't tell Mother, for in disturbing nature and giving myself the horrors I had done something inexcusable and wicked.

I spent only one term at Walthamstow Hall. Mother applied for the prospectus of a private school run by two Frenchwomen. I had misgivings, for it said 'A school for the daughters of gentlefolk', but when I asked if I qualified, Mother smiled rather wryly. Mesdemoiselles Marie and Henriette kept their school, called 'Cambrai', in a large private house in St Botolph's Road, Sevenoaks. It was surrounded by a spacious garden with lawns and woodland and bamboo thickets. I travelled to and from Sevenoaks by train. The school uniform was a violet-coloured tunic, very bright and pretty when new, but the colour quickly faded and became a sickly pinkish grey.

On the first day, in the garden during break I was surrounded by a group of freckled, rosy-cheeked, saucy little
girls, with plaits or ringlets, a few with bobbed hair like my
own. 'What's your name?' On being told my Welsh name they
made faces and tried to say it. 'Have you been christened?'
I shook my head. 'Have you been vaccinated then?' 'No,' I
said proudly, 'my Mother doesn't believe in it.' They danced
round me, 'Mifambly's a heathen, a heathen, a heathen!'
This was bad enough, but then they asked if I had any
brothers or sisters. 'Yes, a brother and a sister—she's very
pretty.' I thought this might endear me a little to them.

'Fancy thinking your own sister pretty!' They danced
round me again. 'What's your father?'

'He wrote books, but he was killed in the war.' At that
they stopped their dance and went off, arms round necks,
whispering. There was one merry little elf-like child called
Brenda whom everyone wanted for a friend. I had noticed
that she scorned the catechising as being boring. Now she
approached me with a peeled golf ball in her hand and was
unwinding some of the tightly wound fine rubber from it.
She asked me if I would like a pennyworth. 'Yes please,' I
answered eagerly, diving up my tunic skirt into the little
pocket of my purple knicker-leg to get out a tiny purse. The
moment I had the elastic in my hot hand I felt its uselessness
and her contempt of me for trying to buy her friendship.

The purple tunics were not obligatory, and I often wore
the dresses with bright embroidery made for me by Mother.
I longed to look like the other girls who when not in uniform
wore navy-blue serge dresses with white collars and cuffs. I
felt conspicuous and began to dislike my unconventional
clothes. In the summer we wore purple and white checked
gingham dresses which could be of any design; mine always
managed to look unusual.

During my first week at Cambrai School the class was

given ten words to learn by heart and then a spelling test a few days later, which we corrected ourselves, each one taking it in turn to read out the spelling of a word. I shone at spelling, so when the child next to me spelt out the word BARON, which I had spelt BARAN, with no hesitation or attempt at subterfuge, I altered my *a* to an *o* and put a tick by it. 'How many have ten right? Hands up.' Mine shot up. 'But Miss Bendle I saw Myfanny alter one of the words when I read out the spelling.' Miss Bendle snatched my book and there was the obvious alteration. 'You have cheated,' said this very old lady in a quavery voice, 'and we send cheats to Coventry.' This terrified me as I thought she was going to send me away from Mother and home. I felt sick and pale. I whispered to my neighbour, 'Where is Coventry?' She put her hand over her mouth, shook her head and pointed at me. I still didn't realise what she meant, though it became clear at break when my class-mates went off in twos and threes, arms clasped round neck and waist, whispering and looking over their shoulders at me.

On some afternoons we did Indian club-swinging to music, which I enjoyed and soon managed well once I had overcome the fear of one of my loosely held clubs flying from my fingers and perhaps crashing through a window. I had, too, a great fear of my glasses getting broken by someone else's club, as I was helpless without them.

Once a week, Miss St Clair came with her accompanist to give us dancing lessons. For these we changed into party frocks with frilly underclothes, white silk socks and bronze kid dancing sandals. The dress I remember best, which of course Mother had made me, was of pale blue Jap silk with three frills from the waist forming the skirt, each frill edged with white swansdown, which could then be bought by the yard. The teacher who supervised our changing made me happy when she said, 'Ah, so you're wearing your

sky-blue-pink today,' and blushing hotly, I spun round to
make the frills fly out. Some of the class wore simple mauve
Greek tunics split up the sides and I noticed it was the more
expert dancers who were unfussily dressed. My peeled
golf-ball friend Brenda was one of them. She was small
and trim in her movements, whereas I was already tall for
my age and rather angular, though very eager to shine at
dancing. Sometimes the class was told to 'rest' while Miss
St Clair picked a girl to show off a step alone—an honour I
longed for. Each Christmas a few of the class were chosen
to dance in a charity matinée in London. They would wear
specially made dresses and dance with flimsy scarves or huge
balloons, but I was never chosen. Eventually Auntie Florrie,
now living with Uncle Ernest and Dick at Otford, made me
a mauve tunic with a beautiful Greek key pattern of narrow
silver braid round the hem. I tried hard to see where the key
pattern had begun, but she had worked out the spacing perfectly and it fitted without the sign of a join. I was a very
critical child, always on the lookout for imperfections.

We had to speak French in corridors and at lunch time
and were not allowed at table to ask, even in French, for a
second helping. One had to nudge one's neighbour and
point surreptitiously to the vegetable dish; if she were
amiable, she would promptly oblige with 'Voulez-vous
encore de pommes de terre?' But someone like the dreaded
red-head Marjorie, with thin face and piggy eyes, would
ignore the hints and one went without. Mam'selle Henriette,
who gave us a lesson in French 'sounds' every day, mostly
looked after the domestic side of the school, and would
pounce on one of us to say grace after lunch: 'Merci, mon
Dieu, pour la nourriture que nous avons prise.' Then we
would all go into a large room with a parquet floor and lie
down flat on our backs, heads on hands, but ankles crossed
were not allowed, while Miss Walters read aloud to us for

half an hour from *The Last Days of Pompeii*. I only liked
the bits about Nydia, the blind girl, because her name
fascinated me. Mam'selle Marie was very fierce when she
found a girl reading *The Girls' Friendly*, a kind of feminine
version of the *Boys' Own Paper* only rather sloppy. With
blazing eyes she snatched the paper from the girl, read out
a few chosen sentences in scornful broken English, and tore
it up. Any more that she found would be *confisqué*. She
had a slight tenderness for me, as I was the only one whose
father had been killed in action, and she was intensely
patriotic. We had a retired sergeant-major to take us for drill
who thumped us in the back if we walked with round
shoulders. He organized a very smart march past on Empire
Day when we all saluted the Union Jack.

There were a few boarders, children whose parents were
in India or working in embassies abroad. For a term three
Chilean children were boarders. Gentle and sweet-tempered,
with pale brown faces and glossy black hair, they were great
favourites. We day-girls envied the boarders when each week
they were summoned in the middle of lessons to have their
hair washed. From the window we could see them sitting in
the sun with towels round their shoulders, eating apples and
reading. Occasionally I boarded for a few days and was
amazed at the difference in Mesdemoiselles Marie and
Henriette, now smiling and friendly. On Sunday mornings
the sisters had a sweet-shop; one could buy a good bagful
for a penny. We would wander all over the big garden, with
its bamboos, sloping lawns and a few splendid trees from
whose low branches one would hang with knees crooked
and read a book.

Soon after the war Mother went walking in the Highlands
with friends during the summer holidays. I stayed with

Nancy Richardson in her cottage near the river. She was
friendly and welcoming and never talked down to children.
I was soon over my homesickness, only crying into my
pillow for a night or two, when Nancy would come and
cheer me up with milk and biscuits.

One morning I woke up hot and flushed, unable to swallow, my throat raw. Nancy produced her universal cure—
senna pods soaked in warm water—and offered me a glass of
the yellow-brown liquid, which smelled sweetish and fusty.
But I couldn't touch it. Dr Dick from Sevenoaks was called,
and in the evening, as it was growing dusk, I was rolled in a
blanket, put into a cab with Auntie Nancy and driven off
into the darkness to the Isolation Hospital, about two miles
away. There I was bundled into the arms of a sturdy nurse
and the cab drove off.

I awoke in the dim whiteness, my throat so painful that
I held the saliva in my mouth for as long as possible to
avoid swallowing. I put out my hand to find my specs—an
automatic movement on waking—and could not find them.
I was burning hot and couldn't understand where I was. It
was very quiet and I could just make out a row of tall
windows opposite me. My arm, which I had slipped from the
bedclothes, looked mottled and puffy and felt hot. I whim-
pered miserably, and soon a buxom country girl bustled in
and said, 'Well, Miffny, how are we? Not very well?' She
told me I had scarlet fever and that we'd soon have me back
home again in no time. I don't remember that first week.
Various tests were made and there was a nightmarish hour
when a glass jar similar to those holding the disintegrating
snakes at the village school, containing samples from me,
was left by my bedside. It made me retch with disgust and
shame, until it was removed by Daisy Scarlet the nurse, who
seemed to spend a great deal of time away from the ward.

In a week or two, when the fever had subsided and I was

able to look about me without that faraway strangeness, I saw that I was in a large ward, empty except for twelve beds in a row opposite me and eleven on my side. At the end of the ward were thick glass doors through which Daisy appeared now and again. When I was able to sit up I could see that these doors led into a lobby where there was a bathroom, a store-room, and a little room where Daisy wrote her notes. Beyond the lobby was an identical ward with twenty-four more empty beds. Daisy told me that Mother had been up to the hospital several times to ask after me and to bring grapes and oranges and my favourite books, but she was not allowed to come into the ward. Scarlet fever was then a notifiable illness and contagious. Mother took the books home again rather sadly, as Matron told her that they could not be taken out of the hospital when I was better. There were a few books in the ward which had been left by other patients, curiously brown after being baked to sterilize them. One was an exciting adventure story called *Cave Perilous* which I read over and over again; and there was another book, lovely and sad, called *A Peep Behind the Scenes*. But my reading or writing time was limited as I was not supposed to use my eyes too much; the rash had affected them too and they were sore and inclined to itch. But I mustn't on any account rub them, Daisy said, or I might go blind. This was terrifying and made me over-cautious.

Sometimes another plump little nurse would come to see mine, waving to me as she passed behind the thick glass door. She was called Daisy Dip. Later, when I could kneel up in bed and look out of the big window behind me, I saw other long one-storey buildings, like my ward. I learned that these were very busy diphtheria wards. There was a serious epidemic which originated from contaminated milk in a village near Sevenoaks. The nurses were worked off their feet, hence my Daisy Scarlet having to give a hand. Tremulously

I remembered that Mother's little brother Philip had died of diphtheria, and that you had to have a knife put down your throat to enable you to breathe.

Matron came in one day, youngish, tall and unsmiling, with high cheekbones and a red face. She said she had a surprise for me. In my dressing-gown and slippers I walked shakily over to the thick glass door and there was Mother, trying hard to smile at the wan, blotchy face peering at her near the glass. It was too thick for us to hear each other speak, so we made signs and touched the glass with our hands, matching fingers. Mother unloaded her basket of goodies for me to see: fruit, eggs, sweets and home-made rock cakes, her speciality. Unable to communicate except by forced smiles and lips pursed for kisses, we waved goodbye.

There was a great bustle one day. All the beds in my ward and in the empty ward next door were wiped down with a wet rag smelling of carbolic. I was moved to a bed in the unfamiliar ward, chilly and echoing, with the fire behind the big nursery fireguard only recently lit. 'You're going to have comp'ny,' said Daisy, not very encouragingly. In the late afternoon a small figure bundled up in a dark blanket was ushered in.

Daisy then took the bundle through one of the doors in the lobby which I had discovered led to a bathroom. I didn't see them emerge and go into the first ward, but a little later Daisy pushed indignantly through the swing door into my ward, red in the face—'Never, *never* did I see such dirt. The first bath he's ever had: the first time he's seen soap and water more like. I've done my best but he's still as black as the ace of spades. Now I'm going to give Daisy Dip a hand.' 'What's his name?' I asked. 'Tom Rose—gipsies, his dad brought him in a pony cart.'

I was sitting up in bed, the ward had not yet got the chill off and the late September evening was closing in, dismal and silent. There was a new view out of my window, and some activity by the back entrance to one of the diphtheria wards. I was horrified to see a small white coffin carried out by two hospital porters in white coats and through the door of a small building, on top of which there was a wooden cross. The chill of the empty ward and my shuddering fear turned me to stone, when suddenly the heavy glass door of my ward was pushed open and a hoarse voice from a small figure in a long white nightshirt below his shaggy dark hair, called out 'Wurr's the noss?' 'Go back to bed,' I said, frightened. 'You mustn't come in here.'

'Wurr's the noss, missus?' I could only think of one thing he might be needing, so I replied, 'Under your bed, go back to your ward.'

'Naow, the noss, the lidy?'

'Oh—she'll be back soon, get back to bed, you'll take cold.' Giving the order, I was conscious of using for the first time an expression Granny always used: always *take* cold, never *catch* it. The door swung to and I could see him exploring the lobby, but couldn't see him go back to his ward. When Daisy returned, her mood was not sweetened when she found the larder door open, the insides of two loaves pulled out, and Tom's bed full of crumbs.

I had been in hospital nearly five weeks and interesting things were happening to the skin on my fingers and arms. It was peeling off in fine dry strips and each morning my bed was full of nasty little dry rolls of skin which had rubbed off in the night. This worried me at first and I said nothing about it until Daisy said, 'That's right, you're peeling lovely. When it's all off you'll be able to go home.' I settled down to read *Cave Perilous* again and enjoyed crayoning the pictures in the painting-book Mother had brought me, though the small white coffin haunted my nights and the dread of Tom, black as the ace of spades, reappearing in my doorway. But I never saw him again.

'Trouble is,' said Daisy one morning, 'you're due out to-morrow, your mum's fetching you in a cab, but your feet haven't finished peeling and you can't go home till that's off.' Daisy had her own methods. That night I was given a very hot bath, wrapped in a blanket and put on a chair by the fire, and while I ate my supper of biscuits and cocoa, Daisy sat with a bowl of hot water and a piece of pumice stone and scrubbed away at my feet, occasionally rubbing off the new tender layer of skin, which drew blood. 'Matron'll grumble at me if she sees this,' said Daisy crossly. 'But I'll see she don't.' This worried me, and I imagined Matron coming round, unsmiling in the middle of the night, to examine my feet and finding them sore would not let me go, or worse still, that I should be allowed home and some-thing terrible would happen because my feet hadn't peeled in their own proper time.

All was well, however, and next day I dressed in the clothes mother had brought the day before and with sur-prisingly feeble legs I went hand in hand with Daisy Scarlet across to the main building and there was Mother. I wanted to rush forward and clasp her, but Matron standing there looked forbidding and Mother looked shy. I took her hand and she prompted me to say 'goodbye and thank you' to Matron. I put out my hand to shake the hand she held out, but it was lifted up to my throat where she pressed my tonsils with cold bony fingers. 'She must have her tonsils removed at once. If she ever gets diphtheria, she wouldn't have a chance.' Mother's eyes looked fierce and she gripped my hand tightly. 'You have no business to say such things in front of the child, frightening her.' 'It's the truth,' said Matron, turning to her office door. 'What did she mean?'

said I, tearfully, thinking of the small white coffin. 'She's a wicked woman.' 'Will I have to have my tonsils out?' 'Not if I can help it—we'll have to see.'

But Dr Dick said the operation wasn't necessary, and I had the rest of term off from school, having lovely things to eat and Virol to build me up.

COMPANY

WITH my eager interest in words and phrases, I loved to hear the village girls say, 'You had company, so we didn't call for you.' That meant we had visitors. But *keeping* company was quite different—if you were keeping company it meant you had a sweetheart and were fair game for teasing. Whereas keeping *you* company was different again and meant companionship when you might otherwise be alone.

Neither Merfyn nor Bronwen was seriously keeping company as far as we knew. They were seldom at Otford. Merfyn was out of the army now and finishing his apprenticeship with the engineering company which made London buses. In later years he was to be a much respected journalist on magazines dealing with heavy vehicles. Bronwen had left school and was living in London, partly with Granny and partly with Auntie Mary, attending an art school where she and our cousin Margaret studied fashion-drawing, and spending much time going to *thés dansants* and musical comedies with Margaret's Uncle Jack or our Uncle Oscar.

Granny came to stay with us quite often, but she did not count as 'company'. I was apprehensive about her visits. She was very little and fragile and now had a glass eye. When I took a cup of tea to her in bed in the morning, I was on edge lest I should see the eye on her bedside table. But of course I never did for she was a very sensitive old lady. She had a way too of gripping my arm when we went out for walks and my long legs had to diminish their stride for her slow steps. Her denouncing of a slut amused us: 'Why, she even shuts drawers with her foot!'

The first real company I recall vividly were Nancy and Lee Henry and their little boy Ivan. Lee was a romantic figure, for he had escaped from a German prison camp, and so could be excused his chain-smoking. He played the piano

beautifully and I would stand beside him and ask for 'I'm
forever blowing bubbles' and 'I'm always chasing rainbows'.
He would play them, with exciting variations and without
stopping, managing to light a new cigarette from the stub of
the one before, screwing up his eyes and holding the cigarette
between his lips. Ivan taught me the words of 'Mademoiselle
from Armentieres'. I thought Nancy Henry very pretty. She
dressed in her London clothes all the time and wore a fur
stole which smelt deliciously of strawberry jam. When he was
not playing the piano, Lee was morose and silent, striding
out for long solitary walks; he had little to say to his timid
son Ivan. He deserted his wife and son soon after, and she
had to fend for herself and the boy, which she did with
courage and enterprise, going round to schools and demon-
strating puppets. She wrote puppet plays and became an
authority on European and Oriental puppets. Later on Nancy
came with Ivan for a hurried weekend. By then she was on
her own and trying to earn her living in London, where for
years after the war ex-soldiers with their medals played and
sang in the street, or stood by a rough old gramophone on a
pram, hunched against the cold in their army great coats.

Nancy was a friend of Polutka and Stephen Hatfield, and
they came to stay with us one weekend. I was enchanted by
Polutka: she had been a dancer at the Polish court before
the war. She had no children and took a fancy to me. I
dressed up and danced for her, and she invited me to stay
in the holidays so that I could go to a proper children's
dancing school which trained juveniles for pantomime and
concert parties. Mother wasn't very happy at the idea of my
going to stay with comparative strangers who seemed to her
rather on the irresponsible side, but I begged to be allowed
to go.

Professor Hatfield and his wife lived in Adelaide Road,
as did Nancy and Ivan. They had a Russian musician friend

staying with them, whom I didn't care for—a cadaverous-looking, tall man, with pince-nez. For the first time in my life I found it necessary to lock the bathroom door when I was washing, as one morning he strode in while I was having my bath and began to shave. This shocked me deeply. Many years later, I saw a photograph in a Sunday paper and thought, '*that* is the man I met and disliked at the Hatfields.' It was Stravinsky. What makes this less impossible is that a ballet company with Karsavina was dancing at the Coliseum: Polutka took me several times, and we saw both *Firebird* and *Petroushka*.

One morning, armed with my ballet shoes and a mauve sateen practice dress gaudily ornamented with gold tinsel, I was taken by Polutka to a dancing-school in a basement near Tottenham Court Road. In a dank cloakroom with concrete floor were a number of little girls in grubby white tarlatan tutus tying on ballet shoes, their skirts spread out behind them, while on pegs where there were as yet no coats, other tutus hung by their shoulder straps. I felt conspicuous in my gaudy tinsel and my spectacles. The children chattered together in rather hoarse but attractive cockney voices. One tiny elegant creature, her skin a warm olive colour, her glossy black hair knotted into a tight coronet above the almond-shaped eyes and high cheekbones, at once attracted my attention. She wore a white leotard with long sleeves and a low neck.

We all sat around the large room waiting for Madame, who walked briskly in, black cane in one hand and a glass of stout in the other. Her tight, black satin skirt and low-cut frilly blouse were set off by the high-heeled, black shiny boots, laced to her knees and just meeting the skirt. Her face was the pinkest I had ever seen, and the astonishing yellow *coiffure* with its coils, plaits and ringlets surmounted by a flat black velvet bow, gave her added height. The pianist with her untidy bundle of loose music followed Madame. She was elderly and peaky-faced, and wore mittens over her swollen chilblained fingers. The olive-skinned girl took pride of place and the rest of us formed in lines behind her for centre work. Tamara, as Madame called her, was often told to face the class and show us various steps and sequences, while we huddled near the barres on three sides of the room to give her more space for her stay turns, double somer-saults, splits and *jetées*. I was sick with admiration and love for this child who moved so lightly and easily, performing the most impossible convolutions of her small, slender body with unsmiling and modest grace. Madame Brown appeared to take no notice of me, but as we were changing after a blissful two hours to go into the dull wet streets again, when these supple children assumed their shabby overcoats and their voices were suddenly very noticeable, she bent over my feet, tut-tutting that already my big toe joints were protruding, as I had been allowed to use my points too quickly. She told me I must massage the joints every day or I should have ugly bunions.

Every other day Polutka came with me and I worked as hard as I could on the barre and tried with the others to touch Madame's glass of stout with the tips of my toes in a high kick—she had to raise the glass very high when it was Tamara's turn—doing *pliés*, the first five positions of arms and feet, and always wondering how incompetent one had to be to get a slap with the black cane.

On the way home we sometimes went through an open air market and once Polutka bought some eels, which I noticed with horror stirred languidly in the newspaper in-side her string bag. In the Underground I tried not to look, in case I should see the black coils slithering out and trying to ooze through the mesh. I watched with shrinking disgust how neatly she flayed the black skin off them in the kitchen sink and how their whitish indelicate shapes writhed still in the bowl of water.

Enchanted evenings were spent watching Karsavina dance *Sylphides, The Firebird* and *Petroushka*. Dressed as a doll, her drawers showing, with round red cheeks and doing the jerky movements, I felt she was wasted in *Petroushka. Les Sylphides* was my dream of what dancing should be: lovely romantic music and the dazzling, white, floating skirts, the glorious patterns of the *corps de ballet*, the strong and handsome prince. And the exquisite ballerina curtseying and receiving so gravely the baskets and bouquets of flowers brought on by gentlemen in powdered wigs and brocade coats. Even when Polutka told me we couldn't after all go round and meet Karsavina in her dressing-room as she had promised, I was not disappointed: I wanted only to think of her in white gossamer with her coronet of rosebuds, her grace and lightness. That night and on many others to come I dreamed of being on a huge stage, no one watching me, invisible music playing and my diaphanous self floating away and away while I danced and leapt about alone.

There was great excitement the following week: Madame was rehearsing her girls for a matinée in a real theatre. Madame Tamara (as she was billed on the programme), dressed in a Turkish outfit, spangled trousers, bare feet with gold anklets, tiny spangled breastplate and long rainbow scarf, was to dance several solos. Then in a dazzling white tutu spattered with sparkling *diamanté* she did spectacular turns, her head twisting as though it were separate from her body. And because I was tall and thin and had straight hair, I was as usual to be a boy. I was to be dressed in a trim tail-coat, top hat and white gloves and to sing a sly song about meeting the girls. I could hardly believe that I was at last to be on a real stage. But I wasn't. Mother came up to see a dress rehearsal and suddenly I had to go back home with her

to Otford; even my tatty practice dress was left behind on
the peg at Madame Brown's. I cried, pleaded and sulked,
but for once Mother was absolutely immoveable—though
she didn't tell me why till much later. She was shocked at
the vulgar little song and the winks and gestures I had been
taught to make while singing it. I suppose there must have
been a fuss with the Hatfields, for we never saw them again.
But the dreams were mine and I thought often of the exquisite little Tamara, the octoroon, whose real name was
Florence. When she grew up she became the wife of Constant
Lambert the composer. He had been captivated by Anna
May Wong, the film actress, and this elegant little creature
closely resembled her.

So back to school again, which had now moved to a much
bigger house on a hill above Sevenoaks and was called
Kippington House, and where Miss St Clair continued to
give us dancing lessons. But it was never the same, I felt a
secret inner superiority that I had had a taste of the real
hard grind of ballet. Anyway, Madame had blamed Miss
St Clair's training for my enlarged toe-joints, which of
course I didn't massage regularly and which I have been
stuck with ever since.
    Much to Mother's amusement I signed the Band of Hope
pledge so that I could join in the 'social' to be held at the
village hall in aid of funds. Miss Violet Underwood played
the piano and talent from all around took part. 'Excelsior'
was dramatically rendered, and I was left wondering what
the 'strange device' was, because these words and the title
of the song were all that I could distinguish. The daughter
of a recently retired vicar—Dorothy's father's predecessor—
who was training to be a singer, sang 'Home Sweet Home'
and 'My ain folk'. She had a heavenly voice, true and

unforced, and looked magnificent in royal blue satin, her
red-gold hair piled high and topped with a matching bow, and
her complexion like wild roses. Strange that this typical
English beauty should have a Eurasian mother who, poor soul,
unvisited and uninvited by the gentry, had become a recluse
and was scarcely ever seen when her husband was vicar.

Dressed as Columbine, all pink tarlatan and rosebuds, I
did my dance, blissfully doing stay-turns and pirouettes to
Miss Vi's playing of Chaminade's 'Autumn'. Then came the
song that I had been waiting for, and which I had seen in
rehearsal, but not in costume. At last we should see something pretty and romantic, for the song was about a dull
little chrysalis who cried because she was so plain and lonely,
and in the end of course 'turned into a butt-er-fly gay!' I
can still hear the strained phrase sung by Miss Browning as
she struggled clumsily out of a long-sleeved cotton over-all,
and on the words 'butt-er-fly gay' stood in a faded green
Sunday dress, with white lace collar. I had imagined great
peacock butterfly wings, with feathery antennae and a bright
silk dress. I felt very sad for Miss Browning. I always expected magic, like the cherries on my hat, and the flying
angels at the children's service. But I always had the warm
and loving—too indulgent, probably—approval and praise
from Mother. She loved things as they were, but I longed
for the unattainable.

She used not to mind when on warm summer evenings I
put on my Columbine dress and moved the gramophone to
the front doorstep, wound it up, put the needle carefully
on the record of 'Valse Triste' and flew down the front
steps to the dusty village street to dance in the moonlight
to the dreamy tune, feeling that my leaps and turns might
lift me up to the stars. The stage to myself, my moonlit
shadow, the record changing magically till my small repertoire was ended—breathless, I went back into the house,

knowing Mother would be there to tuck me up in bed with that wonderfully safe firmness.

Other visitors, including D. H. Lawrence, came and went, and at weekends there was a certain hectic feeling about home: Mother going up to London to have piano lessons, getting to know Sybil Thorndike and her brother, who came to visit their mother in Otford; going to London to see Grand Guignol plays, in which Franklin Dyall, an actor from that 'Bohemian' circle of her young womanhood, took part. She still made most of my clothes and enjoyed gardening and cooking, and reading aloud Dickens, Wilkie Collins, *Treasure Island* and Mrs Molesworth in the evening before bedtime—but she was restless and rootless while I was at school, and anxious about Merfyn and Bronwen having no father to advise and counsel them.

Often Mother would bring back little treasures from Sevenoaks which reminded her of her own childhood: a secondhand copy of *Down the Snow Stairs*, a Victorian children's novel with a strong moral, which I loved and as soon as it was finished begged to have read again; a tiny book with charming steel engravings and bars of music, the book not much bigger than a postage stamp, with a leather binding and in its own velvet box; a set of six tiny wine glasses, with decanter and glass tray all in ruby-coloured glass, just like the set mother and her sister Mary had had for their raspberry vinegar. 'I couldn't resist them!' Mother's eager, loving nature had only me to lavish it upon, and I came, I fear, always to expect lovely surprises when she had gone shopping without me.

Before I leave Kippington House, as leave I had to—the fees went up as the school expanded, and apart from good conversational French, I had learned precious little else—I must speak of a gentle genius, a visiting music master. Mr Taylor, a tall shy man, with a slight speech impediment, used to roar up the drive on his motorbike to give piano lessons and take classes in singing and musical appreciation. In spite of his awkward, diffident manner he had a great gift for teaching and lost his self-consciousness the moment he sat down at the piano. I was completely engrossed during his classes: at my private piano lessons and also during these mixed bags of singing, learning about orchestral instruments, sight-reading, simple theory and composition. One exercise was a particular favourite: Mr Taylor would play a phrase on the piano and one of us had to la-la a response to it. He produced a charming little operetta called 'Marigold', all flowers and fairies, songs and dancing; he trained us and we performed it on the spacious lawns in pretty diaphanous dresses and bare feet.

Suddenly Mr Taylor did not appear for our music lessons, and after a while Mam'selle Marie told us he had been killed in a motorcycle accident.

Now it was decided that I was to live during the week in Tonbridge with my Aunt Mary, Uncle Arthur Valon and my cousin Margaret. They had most generously suggested this arrangement in order to help Mother with her very small income from her widow's and Civil List pensions. I said goodbye to Grisel, all the Mollys and Bettys, Florence and Phyllis, Pavla Plotnikova, Tricia who curled up her tongue in class every day beside me, loosed the gold corrective plate from the roof of her mouth and sucked it with sluicy noises, Brenda who had sold me the golf-ball elastic and who had become my dear friend, Miss Walters, of the sky-blue-pink joke, and poor Miss Bodman, known as the Bodkin, a young woman we tormented in an amiable way and who was the first woman I had ever seen on a hot day with great dark damp patches under her arms and the sticky sharp smell of sweat. Goodbye to Mam'selles Marie and Henriette—'Two pieces of paper are sufficient'—which had interested me on my first day when visiting the lavatory—how can they know? The smell of eucalyptus which surrounded the cold-stricken boarders in winter, the bridges of their noses shiny with vaseline. And the gentle ghost of the music master. Merci mon Dieu pour la nourriture.

MY brother Merfyn was nearly eleven years older than I and my sister Bronwen nearly eight years older. By the time the war was over and Bron had left Bedales and Merfyn was out of the army, they were to me grown-ups. I was very proud of my beautiful sister. Bron loved clothes and had a great many admirers. She had been to all the revues and musical comedies, and powdered her nose even if she were going across the village street to buy a stamp at Top Warrens. I was a little in awe of her and she felt, with reason, that Mother spoiled me. We had been so much together since our father was killed, and I was so terrified of losing her. I know that Mother indulged me and that I knew I could get my way. Her loneliness and restlessness made her very different from my school friends' more conventional mothers.

During those early years after my father's death that Mother and I spent almost exclusively together, I, and I think Bronwen and Merfyn too, felt the same; we never mentioned our father, unless Mother spoke of him, perhaps saying 'Do you remember the time when Daddy . . .'. But on evenings by the fire at Forge House I loved to ask Mother what Bron and Merfyn were like when *they* were little. Merfyn as a very small boy loved to sit on Edward's knee and be told stories or read aloud to, and often his father would read him poems and ballads with words and meaning that Merfyn couldn't understand, but he sat quiet and absorbed, watching his father's face, and when there was a pause while Edward re-lit his pipe, would say, 'Read me about the poetry,' while nursing his tattered rag-doll, Mabel. Mother remembered sitting by the fireside darning, baby Bronwen asleep in her cot, and rejoicing in the happy scene of their first-born on his father's lap, content and alert to the soft grave voice reading a ballad in which the word

'Victor' occurred, when Merfyn solemnly announced, 'I know a boy called Victor.'

I have told earlier about nature walks and Mr Scott at Bedales Preparatory School. Like a number of boys in the early days of the motor car Merfyn was fascinated, and studied all the engines and bodywork details in glossy, coloured brochures. Merfyn had an attractive and mature handwriting and had written for a Rolls-Royce brochure, which he pored over under his desk lid, probably during wet afternoons when Mr Scott, not disposed to take out the lagging boys, was making sketches of trees on the blackboard.

Soon after the arrival of the brochure, a splendid and luxurious motor pulled up by the gate of Yew Tree Cottages while Mother was mending socks in the garden. A smart, town-dressed gentleman came up the path and asked mother if Mr P. M. A. Thomas lived there. Mother said yes, rather doubtfully, wondering what he wanted with Merfyn. 'He has shown great interest in our new model,' said the gentleman, 'And I thought he might care to look her over and take her for a trial run'—he indicated the shining black motor by the gate. 'But my son is a schoolboy and he hasn't come home from class yet!' said Mother blushing and astonished, 'I'm sorry, you've had a journey for nothing.' The gentleman turned very red, bade Mother an embarrassed good-afternoon, and hurriedly returning to the car, drove off.

Merfyn returned from America in time for Christmas 1915, having spent most of his time with Russell Scott and his family, rather than with the Frosts. His journey to the States was a muddle, for the fifteen-year-old boy had to spent three days in primitive conditions on Ellis Island with a number of doubtful characters who were awaiting unlikely permission to land. They were kind to the shy English boy and tried their best to make him feel at ease, among other things teaching him the three-card trick, 'Find the Lady'. I think that must have been where Merfyn learnt the expression 'Snow again, sonny, I don't catch your drift,' which amused his father so much. He loved salty speech, and Merfyn always remembered his favourite story of a cockney father taking his son to the zoo. At the sight of the giraffes the boy said, 'Cor, dad, look at 'is bloody long neck, 'ain't 'ee got a bloody long 'un,' and the father admonishing him, 'Elbert, 'ow often 'ave I told yer not to point.'

In the summer of 1914, while still at Bedales, Merfyn was evidently 'doing' *The Merchant of Venice*, for on the flyleaf of the pleasant little leather-bound 'Temple Shakespeare' edition, is written in his immaculate handwriting:

M. Thomas
19.5.14

P. J. Derkum
C. C. Godfrey
C. B. Franklin
J. R. Alexander
A. H. Alexander
S. George
N. H. Brown
J. T. Bashall

The Indian Team for the T. T. 1914
Result

1st	Pullin	(Rudge)
2nd	(Godfrey	(Indian)
	(Davies	(Sunbeam)
3rd	Colver	(Matchless)
4th		(Triumph

and on the other side:

1. K. Lee-Guiness
2. De Resta
3. A. Lee-Guiness

The Sunbeam Car team for T.T. 1914
Results
K. Lee Guiness

Apart from this the book shows very little sign of use.

In 1916 Merfyn went to school for a term or two at Coventry, where Mr Hodson, a friend of our father's, was headmaster. Merfyn began his apprenticeship as a motor engineer in Walthamstow that autumn, at the same time as the family moved to High Beech, so that both Edward in camp near Romford, and Merfyn at Walthamstow, were within reach of us. Merfyn cycled to Walthamstow early each morning, returning weary in the evening after his day's work. It was here that Merfyn could help his father with mathematics needed for map-instruction and artillery calculations. Merfyn must have enjoyed hearing stories of camp life from his father, particularly the sergeant's comment when he saw a man coiling a rope awkwardly from right to left: 'Were you a snake-charmer before you joined?' My brother had the same enjoyment of dry and salty wit and I was reminded of that story, which Merfyn loved to tell, when I read my father's letters to Robert Frost.

Although she had had two severe bouts of pneumonia as a baby, Bronwen was a sturdy little girl, with corn-coloured hair and large dark brown eyes; her sight was as keen as her father's. She was independent and serene, and would wander off by herself, singing in a rather hoarse voice. She would often be found sitting in the middle of Blooming Meadow at Elses Farm in Kent, making a daisy-chain or sorting out the handful of wild-flowers the names of which she now knew and would soon be seeing if her father could name too, absorbed and oblivious of the bulky presence of the inquisitive sweet-breathed cows blowing at her. She adored her father, and he loved her dearly; she was the epitome of a true country child. She could always jolly him out of a moody silence.

In his lovely poem to her, almost as well-known as 'Adlestrop', he tenderly immortalizes her love of wild flowers:

If I should ever by chance grow rich
I'll buy Codham, Cockridden, and Childerditch,
Roses, Pyrgo, and Lapwater,
And let them all to my elder daughter.
The rent I shall ask of her will be only
Each year's first violets, white and lonely,
The first primroses and orchises—
She must find them before I do, that is.
But if she finds a blossom on furze
Without rent they shall all for ever be hers,
Whenever I am sufficiently rich:
Codham, Cockridden, and Childerditch,
Rose, Pyrgo and Lapwater,—
I shall give them all to my elder daughter.

Not many people realize the implication of the line 'But if she finds a blossom on furze' and also the line in the poem 'October', 'And gorse that has no time not to be gay'. They have their origins in the country saying, 'When gorse is out of flower then kissing's out of fashion'.

Bronwen was often forthright in her remarks about people's appearance, and Mother had warned her about possibly hurting their feelings. It was absolutely all right to remark on, and be curious about, William Davies's wooden leg—'It won't matter if Sweet William is run over by an old cart, because he's made of wood', and stamping on his foot to watch him *not* wince. But others might be more sensitive. With this freshly in her mind, she sat on Ralph Hodgson's lap—he was a great favourite of hers and she of his—gazing up into his face and saying in her gruff voice, 'When I was in London I saw a man with *such* a funny nose.'

She made her father laugh often. Auntie Mary would recall his buying Bron a bag of shrimps, which she was clutching in her fist. The damp shrimps started to come through the soggy bag and fall on to the pavement, when Bron stamped her foot at them saying, 'You stupid old deaf-dumbers!'

Many of my sister's treasures were lost during the Second World War when her things were put in store. Although none of her father's letters to her survived, a page from her autograph album exists, on which he had drawn in dots the constellation of the Lyre and written beneath it:

> This is the constellation of the Lyre:
> Its music cannot ever tire,
> For it is silent. No man need fear it:
> Unless he wants to, he will never hear it.

During the time when Bronwen was staying with Auntie Mary and going with Margaret to the Norland Place School, whenever Edward was in London he would surprise her by waiting on the steps at the entrance; Bronwen would recall that to see him there, tall and smiling, and being lifted up to be kissed, made her day golden, as though they were the only people in the world.

These tales and memories of my grown-up brother and sister enthralled me and I found it difficult to reconcile them with my brother and his motor-bike and my beautiful sister, dressed so smartly and using powder and lipsalve, and regarding me generally as a spoilt, grubby little girl who played hopscotch with the village children or who hung the shavings from the cabinet-maker's plane under her hat, pretending they were curls. But when she came to Otford at weekends she sometimes took me for walks, picking wildflowers and teaching me their names, between whiles singing in her rather quavering and slightly off-key voice, 'There's a little grey home in the west', Tosti's 'Goodbye',

> Dearest, the night is ended,
> Waneth the trembling moon

> Hark how the wind arises
> Dawn will be here too soon . . .

and 'Roses of Picardy'. It was blissful to have her holding
my hand and taking notice of me, so when her songs seemed
to be over I would remind her of other songs: 'Pale hands I
loved' and the cobbler's song from 'Chu Chin Chow'. And
one very sad one, which appealed to me deeply, beginning
'She comes in through the window 'cos the door is not
allowed, Her eyes are like the starlight and her dress is like
a cloud. She holds me very kind and tight and talks about a
lamb . . .', but I could never quite catch the last line and
didn't dare to interrupt.

Sometimes when we were alone I would venture to ask
her about Daddy and she would tell me what a wonderful
person he was. In our wild-flower-picking walks at Eastbury
I asked her if she and Merfyn were ever aware of any tension
at home when Edward was alive. She said firmly, 'Never!'
It was a shock to her when she read in mother's book, *As it
was—World Without End*, that there had been unhappiness
or disharmony; the children were totally unaware of it.

Bronwen is frequently mentioned in my father's letters to
Robert Frost. On 3 November 1915, Edward wrote to Frost:

> Helen, Bronwen and Baba are all collected here (Wands-
> worth) again at my Mother's. It is a London Sunday, and
> the loveliest warm bright weather after a cold bright hazy
> morning that ever was in September. Bronwen and I have
> just walked 4 or 5 miles of streets and crowds. I stand it
> better with her but it is pretty bad—all the mean or villa
> streets that have filled the semi-rural places I knew 25
> years ago.

And in October 1916—just before Bron's fourteenth birthday: 'Bronwen is at my elbow reading *A Girl of the Limberlost*.' He was worried about her round shoulders and she had

to do special exercises, but they were never really cured, nor were her weak ankles.

When Bronwen left Bedales she was at Otford for some months before going to various jobs in London; she soon got to know the presentable young men in the neighbourhood: the vicar's son, who was a medical student, Herbert, a young man who had not much chance as he was too much under his mother's thumb; and Leslie Simmons, who was very dashing in his Royal Flying Corps uniform. She went up to town to matinées with one or other (though Herbert was soon out of the running) to see *The Bing Boys, Kissing Time*, and *Joy Bells*. I heard magical names like George Robey, Delysia, Owen Nares, Adeline Genée and the Co-Optimists. George Robey's name, in particular, intrigued me. Our huge marmalade cat was named Robey; and once when mother was staying with her sister Mary they went to the Chiswick Empire, sitting in the front row of the stalls. Fixing his eyes on Mother, who had not long moved to Otford, pointing at her and shaking his finger knowingly, George Robey said, 'And I could tell *you* something about Sevenoaks!' When he saw Mother's abashed confusion, he added, 'Ah-ha, isn't it funny how he knows!'

I asked Bronwen about musical comedies and I tried to imagine the chorus girls; these appeared in my mind's eye as a row of ladies in dark dresses standing with open sheets of music in their hands. How dull this must be, I decided. So when Bron took me to my first musical comedy, *Irene*, I could not believe that all those handsome young men and gorgeously dressed ladies walking about, joining in the songs in such a carefree way and suddenly dancing with high kicks and swirling skirts, were indeed the chorus.

Mother accepted D. H. Lawrence's advice when she

opened her heart to him about her anxieties over Bronwen's future, and soon she was learning fashion-drawing at an art school in London; our cousin Margaret was also there studying drawing and modelling in clay. But after the discipline of Bedales, Bron was going through a frivolous stage, and did not work seriously. She soon left and became a companion to old Mrs Farjeon—Aunt Maggie—and looked after her and Harry, and occasionally Eleanor too when she was at home.

Aunt Maggie's wardrobe was filled with piles of unopened boxes of chocolates and crystallized fruits, rows of bottles of expensive Parisian scent, unsampled, and dozens of pairs of kid gloves of every length and colour, still folded palm to palm in their pristine tissue paper; all presents which would never be opened, shared, or given away. And yet when he returned home after a long day spent teaching music Harry's supper would consist of a single boiled kipper. But at Christmas, what lavishness! Golden sovereigns in the Christmas pudding as well as silver trinkets big enough to wear round one's neck; the tallest Christmas-tree, loaded not only with real candles and gay little packages, but with spun glass birds, coloured balls, stars and tinsel to delight the eye; then there was Harry's elaborate auction game in which everyone won something of beauty and often of great value. The toy I liked best in the house, which belonged on top of the grand piano, was a little glass box, with a gaily painted scene on the bottom. When you rubbed the glass top with a silk handkerchief tiny paper figures in minute silk kimonos—Japanese I fancy—stood up and moved across the painted scene. Magical!

A terrible thing happened one Christmas. A young teacher lent Eleanor a book which was to be presented to a retiring headmistress. Eleanor put the brown paper parcel with her pile of presents to be opened on Christmas Day. But the book was never seen again. It must have been accidentally thrown into one of the huge laundry baskets where wrappings were put after presents had been opened. The book consisted of contributions by staff and girls—pictures, poems, music —all lovingly drawn or written by hand, bound in tooled leather. The young teacher, who had no business to let the book out of her keeping, was distracted and almost suffered a breakdown. This incident made a great impression on me as a child. We had been brought up to open our presents slowly and not to be greedy and hurry to see what was next.

Our Christmases at Otford were happy ones. Mother loved festive occasions and there was always a wonderful feeling of mystery and expectancy. As the great day approached Mother would be busy stuffing the turkey or opening the oven door to see if the mince-pies were done. Then late on Christmas Eve, when everything was ready, she would ice the cake and Merfyn would put up the holly and mistletoe. On Christmas morning when stockings were opened, the first thing one heard was Merfyn playing the mouth-organ: he had by now added to his war-time repertoire of popular tunes, though the old ones were given an affectionate airing too. The rapture of feeling the bulging angular shape which hung at the end of the bed lasted for years after I had reluctantly come to the inevitable conclusion about Father Christmas.

One year there was a fancy dress dance at the village hall. Bronwen went as a pierrette in a blue and orange outfit, peg-topped trousers, a blue satin top with a wonderful contraption under her arms to hide the hair—in those days respectable girls did not shave—and a very fetching cap trimmed with orange bobbles, as were the trousers. Waiting at the pond for the bus some days later Mother and I overheard two women talking—one was Herbert's mother. A voice rising to a shocked crescendo said, 'And my dear, the whole thing was supported by two shoulder straps!'

Uncle Ernest, Auntie Florrie and Dick now lived in Otford and Uncle Ernest used the 'front room' in their small house for his studio. He did a painting of Bronwen in her pierrette costume and it was used in a series of advertisements for C. B. Corsets in which Bronwen had already appeared several times. Passing the windows of drapers' shops where ladies' undergarments were tastefully displayed, we felt great pride in seeing Bron as the centrepiece, with lacrosse net, hockey stick, tennis racquet, riding whip, dressed for whatever sport she was representing and labelled 'C. B. Girl'. Very occasionally Uncle Ernest used me as a model, when I earned sixpence an hour for smiling blandly and holding a spoon in one hand and an empty bottle of Scott's Emulsion in the other.

Ernest and Merfyn became great friends when the family moved to Otford. They both wore reversed check caps, the peak behind, and went off on their motorbikes to drink together at the Kentish pubs. There was a great occasion at Otford when the Prince of Wales came to hunt with the local foxhounds. Uncle Ernest, Dick, Merfyn, our beloved Uncle Oscar and I walked miles over fields and along lanes in order to see His Royal Highness pass by. On the way we stopped now and then for me to practise my curtsey and Dick his bow. The dazzling smile our party was at last given left a glow in my Royalist heart for many a long day. And after the Abdication Merfyn and I always drank a toast to the King over the Water.

The greatest treat was to be given a ride on the back of Merfyn's Triumph motorbike—LY 345—a cushion strapped on to the carrier or 'flapper bracket' as it was called: girls in their teens were flappers, as they often wore their hair in a thick plait or tied back with a ribbon and on top of this a floppy tammy pulled down on one side. Merfyn had no foot-rests for his pillion passenger, so that I was warned at all costs to keep my legs at a near horizontal angle; otherwise they might get tangled in the wheel, would turn the motorbike over and cut off my ankle all in one go. So gripping the leather belt round Merfyn's waist, my cheek against the disreputable trench-coat, I was ready. Dick would be on the back of his father's motorbike, and Bron in her friend Leslie's sidecar. Having served in the Flying Corps, Leslie wore a leather flying helmet.

Bron and Merfyn spent Saturday evening at the pretty chalet bungalow at the end of the village, built across the river Darenth. This was the home of an attractive young couple, Eve and Henry Arnold, and their baby, known as 'the gadget'. There the four of them danced to the gramophone. Strange to think back to those days now that Henry Arnold's discovery of Fuchs's spying activities at Harwell is legendary. I remember Merfyn going to the Arnolds one evening with an armful of our precious gramophone records; they were put on a radiator and ruined.

At weekends Merfyn sometimes brought Joan Sargent from Sevenoaks on his motorbike, and they would sit holding hands and listening to the gramophone. They didn't seem to mind my being there. She was going to be an exhibition ballroom dancer, but of course had to learn ballet too. Whether Mother, knowing my passion for dancing, had prompted her beforehand, I never knew, but at tea-time she gave the most squalid picture of life in the chorus of a musical comedy, having to sit between performances with feet in hot soda water to keep them from swelling, the crowded dressing-rooms, the poor lodgings and no regular meal-times—and anyway, she added kindly, 'You are so tall and still growing.'

Leslie, from the big house up the lane, spent a good deal of time at the cottage when Bron was there for weekends; he was drinking rather heavily and his mother, although not on 'calling' terms with our mother, had come round to have

an anxious talk about him. Now that he was out of the
Flying Corps, he was not doing any work but living an idle
and expensive life, with his motorbike, matinées and supper
dances. His sister Dorothy, about whom there was village
gossip, was a worry to her mother too. Soon afterwards,
when the Irish troubles were at their height, Leslie joined
the Royal Irish Constabulary as a lorry driver and thence-
forth we saw little of him, though I wrote to him in Ireland.
Bron had other admirers and though I prayed every night
for her to marry Leslie, it seemed pretty hopeless when
she was on the point of becoming engaged to Geoffrey Page.
His sister Kate had been at Bedales with Bron, and married
now to Hubert Foss, a young musician, had come to live at
Eynsford, the next village but one. I could never have
imagined that my rather selfish prayer would one day be
answered—selfish because I thought Leslie very handsome
and because, not being an unqualified success with Bron,
he aimed his affection at me and used sometimes to call
for me at school with his motorbike and sidecar. Twenty
years later he and Bronwen were married.

Lil Snell came to Otford one summer with the hop-
pickers. These unselfconscious, hoarse-voiced strangers from
London's East End invaded the Kentish hop-gardens in
August and September, travelling in special trains. Many of
the families brought all their furniture and household goods
with them to avoid having to pay rent for their rooms
during the six weeks' hop-picking season. The farmer at
Otford housed them in flimsy wooden huts, several families
to each. The Londoners were distrusted and avoided by
the villagers, many of whom also went hopping to earn
a bit of extra money. But the natives kept together in the
heady green alleys of the hop-gardens and did not hob-nob
with the strangers. We were awed by the unusual behaviour
of the women who would crowd round the visiting fish-

monger's cart and amaze us by buying kippers and bloaters which they ate in their fingers, there and then.

Mother and I sometimes spent a day hop-picking, helping Mrs Fordham and Kitty at their bin, getting our fingers golden-stained, and enjoying the busy, friendly atmosphere. I remember a sleepy country-boy being carried home in his weary mother's arms, a wreath of the pretty scented hops round his damp curls, like an infant Bacchus.

Merfyn had a holiday flirtation with Lil, a beautiful Amazonian Cockney, her plaited corn-coloured hair worn like a crown above her blue eyes and russet cheeks. Mother was anxious in case he got involved with some of the fierce-looking men, a few of whom came with their families to pick hops and get fighting drunk on Saturday nights. I remember Merfyn showing us the silver cigarette case he had bought for her, on the inside of which, engraved in his own elegant handwriting, were the words

DON'T FORGET MERFYN

I could see that Mother was troubled, but she said, lightly, 'Oh well, I expect she'll pawn it when she gets home.' Bron looked most disapproving, but I wished Mother hadn't mentioned pawning it, because I thought it was beautifully romantic, and I didn't want it spoilt or to see Merfyn hurt. Perhaps we were all three a bit envious of Lil.

Soon after Lil went home to London, Mother wrote an account of us three children to her girlhood friend Janet Hooton. Merfyn she describes as having standards and ideals to which he sticks and whose instinct is to protect and cherish. Bronwen is irresistible, with admirers wherever she goes but who are treated disdainfully. I was obviously already qualifying for the brief description 'Tall, straight hair and glasses' which remained with me over the years, though Mother thought me quite perfect in every other way!

SCHOOL ON THE HILLTOP

Here on the height of our girlhood's dreamland
Life's way before us lies;
What shall we take as we journey onwards
From schoolday's mem-or-ees?
So shall the school send forth her daughters
Guarding their watchword sti-ill
'Courage and Honour' as England's women
Think of the school on the hill . . .

School on the hilltop
Keep our devotion
True amidst all life's fears:
May our tradition
Of Courage and Honour
Grow GROW G R O W !
With the passing years.

MOTHER and Aunt Mary and I had a spending spree on a green gym tunic, white Viyella blouses, long black stockings, lace-up shoes, house slippers and white gym shoes, navy blue overcoat, and a black beaver hat with green and white striped hatband.

My aunt and uncle had moved from Chiswick to a spacious semi-detached house in a pleasant part of Tonbridge with a lawn and flower-beds at the back which looked over a high wall on to the main Sevenoaks road below. Daisy was the housemaid and Gladys the cook. Uncle Arthur went every day to his office in London, while Aunt Mary and my favourite cousin Margaret led a busy domestic life: making the beds and dusting, shopping in the town, meeting Uncle Arthur at the station in the Renault. Margaret had singing lessons and was Captain of the Girl Guides; she played tennis, made her own dresses and painted in her spare time. Tonbridge was a new world for me, prosperous and well-ordered.

For school in the morning I shared a taxi with Meg from next door and we walked home together in the evenings. The County School stood at the top of a long hill, in spacious playing fields—very large and regimented compared with my previous easy-going French school. The cloakroom with its rows and rows of pegs beneath which were wooden benches was reminiscent of Walthamstow Hall, though here I was not teased, but the row of wash-basins and lavatories beyond filled me with the same disgust at the messy state they were nearly always in by midday.

There was a proper gym with sprung floor, ropes, rib-stalls, buck and horse, and you tucked your tunic into matching knickers for more freedom. Miss Featherstone, an Old Girl, was the gym mistress, and wrote down in a book the week when one could be excused from doing gym and no nonsense. Hockey was played, as well as netball. Hockey frightened me because of my glasses and the way the ball came at your face, and I could never hit it or get out of its way quick enough, and soon begged my aunt to write a note excusing me from playing. So I played netball instead, or tried to, but even with the big leather football I didn't seem able either to catch or dodge it, so that I was con-stantly getting it in my face and my specs were almost permanently on the skew. There were goddess-like creatures who were prefects and told you not to run or talk in the corridor, Amazonian Joan Tompsett and Enid Tasman were my special favourites. Noreen, the Head Girl, was tall and austere, with her hair done up and, because she looked like a teacher, except for her green gym tunic, quite unapproach-able. Joan and Enid sometimes gave a glance that was almost a smile and then our cheeks flushed with pleasure and we walked down the long corridor on air.

The christian names at the School on the Hill were on the whole more homely and conventional than the Delphines, Pavlas, Katrionas and Grisels of the Sevenoaks school—there were dozens of girls called Gladys, Margery, Betty and Molly, Joan and Janet, Kathleen and Dorothy—and one merry girl, very good at games and gym, called Amelia Jane Buggs—or Millie. There was the occasional Myrtle, Charlotte, Grace and Ruby, and Phyllis, too, names seldom seen these days on a school register. Every year a number of clever girls from village Board schools won scholarships and came by train from Penshurst, Paddock Wood, Horsmonden and Hildenborough. They were known as the Scholarship Girls, and they had to leave promptly to catch trains home, while the rest of the class might be kept in a quarter of an hour beyond the home-time bell for being inattentive. One of the young mistresses who took us for mathematics, scribbling tiers of figures on the board and explaining a method with her back to us, was often scornful of the scholarship girls, inferring that they had come there on charity. This filled me with embarrassment and dislike, for I knew that I could never have passed an exam to get a good education, especially from a village school like the one at Otford. (It was odd, too, that this teacher was the only person in the whole school who wore a red rosette at election time.) I sat behind a very clever scholarship girl called Nora Woolger. She had thick, tight plaits, braided with four instead of the usual three strands, and a little curl in the nape of her neck.

I had great difficulty in concentrating or applying myself and was often completely unaware of what the lesson was about, especially geography. Trade winds and their direction were my particular bugbear. If only we'd been told why they were called trade winds I could have imagined those tall ships bringing back their spicey cargoes from the East,

the winds filling their sails and speeding them home to
Bristol and Liverpool. History too seemed to be all about
Acts, which we had to learn, and the terms of Treaties after
wars. French lessons were an acute embarrassment because
I had acquired a passable pronunciation at Cambrai, and if
I used it when reading aloud I felt a show-off, so that the
one subject in which I might have shone, had to be dimmed
and anglicized. One day when it was my turn to read aloud
from a French classic and then translate the passage which
was about some sailors who were half-naked, Dorothy, who
was sharing the book, whispered, 'Which half?' which I
thought common. But poor Dorothy looked so abashed
when I didn't respond that I smiled rather weakly, for to
be stuck-up was the worst possible bad form. English I
loved and I wrote long, rambling, romantic stories about
cowboys and Spanish ladies in mantillas with roses between
their lips, or the adventures of a sixpence, which conveniently
ended down a grating in the road.

I would get home in time for tea in the drawing-room
with Aunt and Margaret, a three-tiered cake-stand, a brass
Indian tray on a carved wooden stand set with the silver
tea-service, a special little pot of Indian tea for me, while
Margaret and Aunt had Earl Grey. A delicious meal to be
lingered over in order to put off the moment when I must
set about my homework. We were supposed only to spend
half an hour on each subject—a senseless rule, for if we had
not finished the exercise when we handed in our work, we
had to stay in after school and complete it. If the subject
were arithmetic, I sat in the morning-room after tea, staring
at the problem of taps filling baths with the plug out,
having no idea how to tackle this apparently insoluble
problem. Thanks to my patient cousin I had at last grasped
the method of long division and long multiplication of
pounds, shillings and pence, but problems, vulgar fractions

and decimals were another matter. I felt I ought to be able at least to make a start, but in the end I would appeal to Margaret. She was always willing to have her singing practice interrupted. Sometimes, if Margaret were out, I had to wait until Uncle came home from town and had had his glass of sherry with a water biscuit, and then he would show me—though his method was quite different from the one I had been 'taught' but had not understood. Uncle's words for setting out the problem seemed a little archaic, and would be spotted by the eagle eye of the maths teacher. Flushed and hot-eyed I would still be poring over the books when Uncle had changed into his dinner-jacket and Margaret and Aunt into semi-evening dresses and the gong had sounded for dinner. Then I went into the dining-room for soup, my Aunt serving it with a silver ladle from a great silver easter-egg of a tureen, with a magic lid that disappeared when slid open. I carried my soup into the morning-room where Daisy had left a tray with a roll and butter and some fruit. I was supposed to be on my way to bed before they came out of the dining-room for coffee. Daisy would tip me off: 'They'll be out in five minutes, Miss.' And when Aunt had finished her coffee, which Uncle made in a Cona coffee-maker over a methylated spirit lamp, she would come up to say 'Nightee good wishee no time for kissee' and I would say 'Nos da y chwi' as my father had always bid me goodnight, and Aunt would give me a hug and tuck me up, letting me read for a bit before I put out the bedside light.

Aunt Mary loved entertaining and often old school friends of Margaret's would come and stay for a week, which I enjoyed too. Sometimes Mother's and Aunt Mary's elder sister Irene would come; we were on tenterhooks most of the time because of the arguments which nearly always arose. My uncle teased her outrageously. Aunt Irene had just been accepted into the Jewish faith and my uncle would

say, 'I won't offer you any bacon at breakfast, Irene,' and
my Aunt would say, 'Oh, but I belong to the reformed Jews.'

Uncle Arthur was one of a large family of brothers and
sisters, most of whom were married and prosperous, and
when they visited the comfortable house at Tonbridge,
they generously accepted me as another niece. At that time
only two members of the family had children, Uncle Arthur
and Auntie Belle, who with her jolly husband Uncle Harry
had two sons of about Margaret's age, one in the Navy and
one at Cambridge. Then there was Auntie Kitty with her
sailor husband, who had had exciting adventures at sea;
Auntie Ethel, unmarried; Uncle Willie, small and plain
among his comely brothers and sisters, ruled by his mother-
in-law who shared his home. To our great amusement Uncle
Willie always referred to his wife as Mrs Valon, even to his
own brother. Our favourite was Uncle Jack, debonair and
full of charm, an elegant bachelor and perfect dancer, who
took Margaret and sometimes Bronwen to *thés dansants* and
musical comedies. He was very like Jack Buchanan both in
looks and stage-manner, which endeared us to him even more.

Lastly there was Uncle Charley who had been wounded
in France in the war and was paralysed. His devoted wife
was always ready to help him from his wheel-chair to an
upholstered one, and to cut up his food, which he could
manage to eat with a fork in his white, listless fingers. He
was very handsome and fragile, with a gentle humour.

Aunt Mary loved having her house full; she provided
delicious meals, and Uncle Arthur or Margaret took their
guests for drives in the Renault. Their's was a comfortable
world where daughters had dress allowances, and were not
expected to leave home and earn a living, where friends
were always made welcome; dinner was by candlelight, and
there was a finger-bowl beside one's plate. Everything was
planned and ordered and ran like clockwork.

When I went home every other weekend, it was to another world: Mother would be cooking or working in the garden, Merfyn and Bronwen's friends arriving unexpectedly and having to shake down on the divan in the sitting-room, the late rising on Sunday, when instead of roast beef and York-shire pudding we would have 'brunch', with poached eggs on smoked haddock, tea, lashings of toast and marmalade and a slab of Mother's home-made gingerbread. After this the men would go over to The Bull for beer or take their girls out on motorbikes.

Bron was now engaged to Geoffrey Page; she looked after his sister Kate Foss's two little girls at Eynsford. Sometimes I went to Eynsford at the weekend and stayed in the crowded cottage. Hubert Foss had many musician friends, some already making their names as composers—Philip Heseltine (soon to call himself Peter Warlock), Van Dieren, Moeran, and a delightful singer named John Goss. Francis Meynell was often of the party. *The Week-End Book* had not long been published, and afternoons—between pub opening times—were spent playing and singing the sea-shanties and folk-songs in the book, with their roaring choruses. I felt uneasy in this company, knowing they were speaking about things they didn't want me to hear. They used a kind of second language which made me feel shy and discomforted, no longer a child but too young for grown-up jokes.

I experienced the same guilty feeling when a friend was reading James Joyce's *Ulysses*, then banned in England, aloud to Mother. Occasionally he read a passage in French, which I understood perfectly and felt miserable and deceit-ful at not saying that I did; but I was more shocked that books should print what I felt to be disgusting and private; and worse still that my Mother should be subjected to this, as she looked most uncomfortable.

At Eynsford I was glad to get away from the noisy cottage

and visit Mrs C. E. M. Joad and her two demure little girls at
the end of the village. She was quiet and conventional and I
felt easier in her company. Mother was to have a room in the
Joads' house in Hampstead while the nervous illness resulting
from Edward's death was being treated.

At this time Mother rested a good deal. She had lost her
warm colouring and her vigorous eagerness. If she were resting
upstairs the sound of Merfyn's jazz records distracted her
and she would plead for the gramophone to be turned off.
Bron's fiancé, Geoffrey, had recently had a crash on his
motorbike. He had fractured his skull and was in hospital
for months. His illness and Bron's distress added to Mother's
feeling of inadequacy. She resented her own loss of vitality
which should have been available to comfort and sustain
Bronwen.

I hated parting from Mother. Her unaccustomed languor
and intolerance bewildered and distressed me. Yet it was
almost with relief that I got back on Sunday evening to the
orderliness of my aunt's home. I kept a close guard on what
I said about Otford and Eynsford for I sensed my aunt's,
and particularly my uncle's, disapproval of our rather hap-
hazard way of life. I kept my two very different homes
entirely separate.

As a great treat Margaret and I would go to the pictures
together, always with a bag of Fox's glacier mints, to see
Mary Pickford, Lilian Gish or Rudolph Valentino in ro-
mances, spectaculars like *Ben Hur*, and a glorious serial
called *The Jungle Goddess* where each episode ended with a
close-up of the heroine running, level with the camera,
looking over her shoulder at the gorilla, witch-doctor or
lion which was chasing her. What I wanted to see most was
The Hunchback of Notre Dame, but it was considered unsuitable, and I have never seen it. There was an added
glamour in going to the cinema, as we schoolgirls were not

supposed to go and were expected at weekends always to wear our school hats so that we would be recognized.

My hosts were very fond of the theatre, particularly romantic musical comedies, especially if Evelyn Laye played the heroine. They saw *Madame Pompadour* several times, and bought records of some of her songs:

Joseph, O Joseph, Why are you so coy?
Do have a dash at me, you bashful boy.
O Jo-Jo-Jo-Jo-Joseph, you cold and cruel man
How much you miss of earthly bliss
Why don't you kiss me while you can?

It was on one of these occasions, when the family spent the night in town and I was in the charge of Daisy and Gladys, that Gladys, at my blushing request was crocheting me a bust-bodice, though she said, 'It's two pudding basins you need, Miss.' I felt that wearing the quite unnecessary garment might encourage the swelling bust which I so envied in girls of my age. That night I had supper with the maids in the cosy kitchen and before I went to bed, Gladys tore up a piece of old sheeting from Daisy's polishing rags and rolled my hair, which I was growing at the time, into tight curlers. I was enchanted, but I slept only fitfully that night, thinking of the corkscrew curls which would bounce round my ears in the morning. I had my breakfast in the lonely dining-room and then with brush and comb I went to the kitchen for Gladys to undo the curl-rags and brush each ringlet round her finger. The effect I thought very attractive, particularly the feel of the stiff ringlets when I tossed my head. I was late for school, and breathless and red in the face walked into the Physics Lab where the first lesson took place. Miss Pomeroy, the science teacher, was an unemotional lady with a face rather like a rosy toad, with straight, red, moist lips. I apologized breathlessly for being late and went to my place, feeling the eyes of the class upon my lively curls. Miss Pomeroy was bending over her lesson notes and merely nodded at the interruption. As I settled myself on the stool by the bench with sinks and bunsen burners, she looked up and without apparently addressing anyone in particular said complacently, 'Go and plait your hair, M. Thomas.' In the hush following this order, I hurried from the room, hot cheeks and stinging eyes bent low over my green tunic, and rushed for the cloakroom. Snuffling and sniffing, with shaking hands, I tugged at my hair with a comb and finding a pair of old plimsoll laces in my shoe-bag, managed to tie it up in two frizzy bunches over each ear. When I returned to the lab, nothing more was said to me until the end of the lesson when the moist red lips said, 'Get the notes from D. Outram.'

The family was home again by the time I got back. By this time my hair was in a tangled muddle. Seeing my aunt's smiling face, I burst into tears, put my head in her lap, and told her the story. She stroked my head gently, saying, 'How unkind of Miss Pomeroy.' I probably didn't say that I had been late for class.

Margaret's cousin at Cambridge had given the family tickets for the Footlights Review, when Norman Hartnell and Cecil Beaton were involved in the production. It was the time when Eton crops and long cigarette-holders were in fashion. When Norman Hartnell set up as a dress designer, Margaret went to his first fashion show and her parents bought her a beautiful romantic 'picture' dress, made of tiny frills of rosebud-sprinkled taffeta, each frill edged with a tiny rouleau of china blue silk.

One weekend I went home to Otford and saw that the road outside Forge House had been strewn with straw. I rushed in at the front door and Bronnie greeted me with her finger to her lips. I felt panic-stricken at the sight of the straw and was told it was to deaden the sound of the horse traffic in the road. Mother had come to the end of her tether and any noise was agony to her. She lay in bed, pale and unresponsive. Merfyn and Bronwen and their friends spoke in whispers. The doctor had said she must get away, meet friends, buy a new hat. As soon as she was able and when friends had found her lodgings near Eleanor in Hampstead, she went to stay in the Joads' house in the Vale of Health on Hampstead Heath, next door to a derelict house— one of six tall Victorian terraced villas. The social life, with theatres and shopping expeditions would take her out of herself, the doctor assured her. Eleanor, who now had a great friend, George Earle, with whom she had visited us at Otford, had written enthusiastically to Mother: how lovely it would be to have her near, to be able to do something for her in the way of theatre-going and parties. A schoolmaster with a single-minded passion for Keats, George Earle had met my father briefly when he was a soldier. George had been holding forth about Keats and had made a slightly contemptuous remark about soldiers not having any interest in poetry. He couldn't recall a quotation from one of the Odes and without looking up from his book, the quiet corporal smoking his clay in the corner provided the lines. I always disliked Pod, as George Earle was called—he expected children to kiss and be fondled and to sit on his knee.

Mother found rest from the noisy Forge House, where Kate Foss and her children spent much time. Kate had constant tussles with her first child who had terrible nervous screaming fits, which only Mother could soothe. But soon Helen was overcome by bouts of excruciating pain which would suddenly wrench her body. Each specialist she visited, looking at his watch as lunchtime approached, would recommend her to come to his nursing-home and he would operate for gall-stones or whatever particular ailment he specialized in. Mother resisted these invitations as she had shrewdly noticed how little the consultant had asked her about her symptoms, and how when she described them he had scarcely listened. She had almost given up hope when she heard of a Portuguese-Irishman, Dr Sorapure, who was not on the medical register. She went to see him and he listened to her. He started a long course of treatment at the Joads' house, which eventually cured her.

Now that Mother was for the time being staying on in London, Kate and her family, with Hubert only occasionally with her, and accompanied by a French Mademoiselle Marie Thevenet, moved officially into Forge House as temporary tenants.

My homesickness for Mother, now far away and ill, was acute: I was growing very fast—my uncle called me a painted maypole. My aunt insisted that I should take a term off school as I was 'outgrowing my strength'. I had had measles very badly and was rather 'seedy', as my aunt described my general lassitude. I have never been able to overcome a slight disgust at the use of the word 'seedy'. Mother always said 'poorly', a North Country expression which I liked, but 'seedy' produced an image of a collection of dark, pointed seeds, closely pressed together.

However, I enjoyed being able to go shopping with my aunt, and every day to have a delicious lunch of crisp rolls, cream cheese and bramble jelly. Because I was so tall and thin I now had dinner in the evening, changing my dress and learning to use the finger-bowl and how not to hold my spoon like a drumstick, as my uncle told me. I went for drives with Margaret in the Renault, and watched her at the Sevenoaks folk-dancing classes she attended. Once I went to Winchester to stay with one of Uncle's sisters and her family. I read a great deal: *The Blue Lagoon, The Forest Lovers,* and

Bulldog Drummond novels, helped Margaret with her Girl
Guide work and studied for the badges with which my uniform sleeve was becoming pleasantly covered. It was glorious
not to be at school. I don't know why I disliked it so much:
I got on reasonably well with the teachers and the girls. I
resented the fact that as I came from a literary family I was
expected to be good at English. To be marked down as good
at things was despised, unless it was at games, and that I
never was.

I suppose my aunt, wrongly as it turned out, felt that my
languor was the forerunner of my physical development, and
she rather surprisingly gave me the plays of a Frenchman to
read. Their theme was the wages of promiscuity. One I particularly remember was *Damaged Goods*. I was hurt and
shocked by these plays and wondered what I was supposed
to do when I'd read them. I decided to put the book back in
the shelf. Perhaps my aunt thought better of whatever she
had had in mind, because she never referred to it again.

Always cheerful and making light of her long illness,
Mother kept in touch with me through her wonderful
letters. Very occasionally I went to see her at weekends.
But more often at first I went to Otford. Geoff was still
convalescing from his accident and Bron was looking after
a child in London, in order to be able to go and visit him
at his home at Winchmore Hill. Merfyn was quite often
at Otford for weekends, and the French girl, Marie
Thevenet, carried on a mild flirtation with him, though she
was faithful to her Maurice in Paris. One weekend, when
Kate and her friends were over at The Bull, Marie asked me
to take her photograph to send to Maurice. After a few
minutes she came out of the back door, where the dustbin
and coal-shed were, clad in a chiffon chemise and carrying a
looking-glass. She stayed very near the back door, where the
light was poor. It was sheltered from any passers-by and

with my box Brownie I snapped her in various poses, smiling archly into the looking-glass. When the film was developed, Mademoiselle's saucy transparent underwear might have been made of stout calico. Poor Maurice!

I felt out of place at these weekends unless Merfyn were there. He kept a brotherly eye on me and managed to get me out of the way if any of Kate's friends were drunk. I was apprehensive too following the time when I had run upstairs to hide from John Goss the singer, who was 'He' in a game of Hide and Seek. I wedged myself against the bedroom door, only to find when I turned round that young Harry was sprawled on my bed in one of his frequent stupors after drinking at The Bull. Harry was a handsome Cockney boy whom Kate had befriended. He was said to be a doomed man, a murderer who had turned informer. Another time I came across him in the coal-shed, lolling grey-faced among the logs and coal-dust.

The musicians from Eynsford, sometimes joined by Francis Meynell, and most of them accompanied by girls, came over on Sundays for a game of rounders in the recreation ground. The girls meanwhile lazed about at Forge House, talking in drawling voices about their menfolk. They all looked much alike, with rather long, loose hair, and long, low-cut dresses of a nondescript pond-colour, and each, I thought, in need of a good scrub, hair and all. These casual guests with their noisy singing and amorous dalliance, interspersed with the elder child's screaming fits, discouraged me from visiting the cottage. I had noticed my mother's precious books lying about and that several of her cherished ornaments had been chipped or cracked, or were missing.

I have to keep in mind that at this time (1923) my father's poems had been published in roughly two halves, in a thin volume a few months after his death in 1917 and the rest in 1918. A small edition of his *Collected Poems* appeared in 1920. They were then known only to a few readers, so that the following rare personal encounter with the headmistress of my school had a salutary effect on me. I had never possessed a copy of his poems and only knew vaguely those he had sent to me from camp, which Mother had read to me.

I had returned from my term's release taller and thinner than ever and at once felt very behindhand with all the work that had been done in my absence. The Headmistress took us for Scripture; we were doomed to study either the Old Testament prophets and tribal wars, or St Paul's missionary journeys. These journeys involved the dreaded drawing of maps from blackboard sketches with illegible chalked place-names and little dotted lines in different colours to show the routes and towns St Paul had visited on his travels. My maps tended to end up looking like pieces of knitting which a kitten had played with. Once for our homework we had to write an essay on one of the Old Testament lessons. After much sighing and pen-chewing I was relieved to find I had managed to cover, with ample spaces between words, the required minimum of a page and a half, on wars, their causes and effects, all quite incomprehensible to me. A day or two later I was sent for by the Headmistress: with dry mouth and my heart knocking, I tapped on her study door. No response. Hope surged that she wasn't there and I would be forgotten. I tapped again. This time an impatient shrill voice commanded, 'Come in.'

'Ah, M. Thomas.' She swivelled round in her chair to face me, my Scripture notebook in her raw-looking hands. 'What does all this mean?' she asked. I waited some moments with burning face before replying. 'Please, I don't know.'

'I find you have used the words "the people" thirteen times. *What* people?'

'I don't know.'

'Your father has written a fine poem about Words. Do you know it?'

'Not really.'

'Come, either you know it or you do not.' Silence. 'You should read it, get to know it. He has a sensitive feeling for words and their use and meaning; in one line he says, "Use me, you English words" as though he wished them to use him as their faithful vehicle. "A language not to be betrayed" he says elsewhere.'

'Yes, Miss Fayerman.'

'Do you think your father would feel proud of the writing in this essay? What would he have thought of this worthless piece of nonsense?'

'Please, I don't know.'

'You will do it again, this evening, and hand it in to me tomorrow morning.'

'Yes, Miss Fayerman. Thank you,' I said, taking the wretched book from her and walking across the study, feeling as though it were an endless expanse, her large light blue eyes behind her rimless glasses on my faded outgrown tunic and black stockings. I went back to my classroom, burning with shame and resentment, anger and misery, that I had so let my father down. But I did read the poem, and something of my father's pleasure in a language not to be betrayed flooded into my mind and heart. I found that I could now read more critically and enjoy the rich sound of words.

I began to read my father's poetry, and had deep satisfaction when I came across those poems in which some words or actions of mine were woven into the poem, and I felt a small part of its creation. For although I knew *I* was part of my father's own unique creation, I had always rather resented the poem that he had written for me: it perpetuated what I longed to be without—my spectacles, my straight hair, my acquisitiveness. True, he had called my hands small, which was tender; but even so, I felt he had accentuated the chinks in my armour and couldn't therefore have liked me as much as the others—Merfyn his first-born and Bronwen his beloved smiling one, who answered him cheekily and who had had eight more years of knowing him than I had. But I recognized myself in 'Old Man', 'The Cherry Trees', 'The Brook' and I remembered the occasion of our seeing together 'The Gallows', and 'Out in the Dark'. And only recently, in my seventies, with grown-up grandchildren, have I discovered that I am the child in 'Snow':

> In the gloom of whiteness,
> In the great silence of snow,
> A child was sighing
> And bitterly saying: 'Oh,
> They have killed a white bird up there on her nest,
> The down is fluttering from her breast.'
> And still it fell through that dusky brightness
> On the child crying for the bird of the snow.

The poems, in their grave austerity, did not appeal to me as did the warm and sensuous Odes and sonnets of Keats, or the anguish of Shakespeare's love poems, but I felt that something had become more whole in my being and the poem 'Words' which astonishingly my cold headmistress knew and understood, I read again and again—'Use me, you English words.'

Mother had now recovered from her long nervous illness, caused by delayed shock, and had decided to settle in London. She bought the semi-derelict house next door to the Joads. It was patched and painted, and soon bright with gay curtains and carpets, and our Otford furniture, augmented with things she bought from the Caledonian market.

I went to London for weekends and holidays, and Mother and I went to the theatre, to music halls, revues, and the haunting German film *Warning Shadows*.

We took a school-friend from Sevenoaks—Brenda of the golf-ball—on holiday to Wimereux; from there Mother went to see Edward's grave at Agny. I remember watching a fire-eater in the market-place. Two burly peasants strode into a space, spread some dirty matting on the cobblestones; one filled his mouth from a bottle, put a match to his lips, and blew out flames several feet long, afterwards spitting beside the mats and wiping his blackened mouth with a sweaty hand. The second man then proceeded to tie the other man's hands and feet, threw him roughly on the mat, and, opening an old 'Gold Flake' cigarette tin scooped up from it three languid and sick-looking snakes which he flung on to the prone man's chest where they stretched and writhed while he struggled out of his knotted ropes. On our last day by the sea, we saw a drowned English girl being landed from a fishing boat; her tallow-coloured face and straggling hair haunted me long afterwards.

Geoffrey had now completely recovered from a fractured skull and he and Bron were married from our aunt's house in Tonbridge. They were to live on the first floor of the tall house in Hampstead. Mother would have the second floor, while Merfyn and I would each have a room at the top of the house. Mrs Bentley was to be our cook-general. With her husband and two children she would live in the basement.

A few days before the wedding in July 1924, Mother wrote to her friend Janet Hooton:

> My dear old Janet
>   It is very sweet and forgiving of you to write to me on my birthday, and I was very touched by it, and write

at once to thank you. Tho I put my own address at the top I am really staying with Mary who now lives at Tonbridge and we are all in a state of tremendous excitement and bustle and happiness, over Bronwen's wedding which takes place on Tuesday next. You were down on the list of those to be invited, but I could not remember or find out your address. However, tho I've not got the proper printed invitation with me please take the will for the deed.

Bronwen is marrying Geoffrey Page—an old Bedales friend, the son of Carter Page the seed people—a very nice boy whose greatest recommendation to me is his utter devotion to Bronwen to whom he has been engaged for three years. He is 23 and she is 21 so they will start young and in a humble way, tho when I think of how I started, in comparative luxury. Bronwen is very pretty and he is a very nice looking boy tall and fair, and both are extremely smart, so that as far as looks go the affair will be very pretty. She's got a lovely trousseau, and is having lots of beautiful presents. They are going to share a house with me in Hampstead where I am moving in the Autumn. I have been awfully ill—a sort of long drawn out nervous break-down, the result so the doctor told me of the shock of Edward's death in the first place. In fact since then Janet life has been so difficult for me that I've often and often felt I could not bear it any more. I can't resign myself to things at all—grief and despair and loneliness swept over my soul again and again leaving it shrivelled, and my life so dependent on my affections has had nothing to cling to, but has been lost and wandering. Friends have been lovely to me giving me love and help and encouragement, and my children are all I could desire, but always always always I need and long for my lover to whom I gave my whole being, and in giving myself possessed myself as I can never do again.

But now after terrible times I am much better, and perhaps life will become calm, tho just at this time how I turn to Edward and miss him and long for him. Well, life never was easy for me—I am too tossed here and there by my emotions.

But no more of myself. Merfyn is 24, and doing *awfully* well as a motor journalist. He's just got a rise and is very well and happy. Myfanwy lives during the school term with Mary, spending her week ends with me. She's tall and lanky and the most like Edward, mentally I mean.

Mary and Arthur are *very* prosperous and things go easily with them as they always have. They are very kind and jolly, and are having the wedding from this house and doing it in great style.

How I wish my dear I could get to see you, well, I'll try one of these days. How splendid Aunt Emily and Uncle Arthur [Janet's parents] are wonderful old people. Little Bronwen has no father or grandparents on my side to see her married, but Granny Thomas still goes strong, tho Mr Thomas is dead. . . .

With her usual dauntless courage, Aunt Mary, unknown to anyone, was postponing a grave operation until the wedding was over. It was a happy day in July. Bron was dressed in beige, the newest colour, with orchids to match from the nursery run by Geoffrey's father, Carter Page. Margaret and I as brides-maids carried tight Victorian posies and Merfyn flirted happily with Gladys and Daisy, smiling in their new frilly caps and aprons with sprays of white heather pinned to their bibs.

A month or two after the honeymoon Bron and Geoffrey came to their new home in Mother's house and had a short, gay life together, dancing and theatre-going; but on a bitter day in the new year, Merfyn came to Tonbridge to give me the news of Geoffrey's death from pneumonia.

Bron was taken on holiday to Italy by Geoffrey's sister, Kate, and other friends. There she had a strange experience, which she often recalled, as she was destined to lose her three husbands from illness. At a Venetian restaurant where they were dining a guitar player came round the tables singing. After a while he asked if any lady would like to lend him her wedding or engagement ring, and he would tell her fortune. Kate persuaded Bron, much against her will, to lend her ring. The gipsy had foreseen happy lives for other women, with large families of children, riches, travel. But when he held Bron's ring in his palm, he gazed at her and shook his head and would tell her nothing.

When she returned from Italy, still bemused by loneliness and at twenty-three quite untrained, she worked with a friend in a smart milliner's shop in St James's, off Piccadilly. She would meet her friends for lunch in 'Sandy's, one of the first sandwich bars, which was run by Kenelm Foss, one of Hubert's brothers. It was close to the Prince of Wales Theatre, and occasionally at the weekend I would meet Bron at the theatre and together we would go to see one of Charlot's revues. Gertrude Lawrence, Bea Lillie, the stars, and Jessie Matthews who was in the chorus. Now that I was growing up Bron and I were much better friends.

My aunt was away in a nursing-home in London until she had completed a course of radium treatments. When she came home her oval face was drawn and pale, and I was frightened of bumping into her, so clumsy and gawky was I at that age. But she still came to tuck me in at night, though I felt I must no longer hug her tightly for fear of hurting her. She told us how careless of their own safety the nurses were with the radium in the leaden box, and how she begged them to take as much care of themselves as they took of their patients.

At this point memories are suddenly crowded and the chronological order is hazy. I remember a visit with my uncle and aunt and Margaret to their relatives in Winchester, and the straight Roman road on which we travelled. There I had my first ride in an open sports car, as Margaret's cousin owned a Bugatti, its bonnet strapped down with buckled leather. Margaret was in another car with my driver's brother; it was tailing us, but suddenly it was not there and though we waited it did not catch us up. 'I wonder what can have happened?' I said anxiously, but my driver answered, casually, 'Oh, they'll be having an osculating match.' (I had to look that word up in the dictionary before I could be sure of the meaning.)

I went on a visit to Paris with six or seven other girls from school, in the care of two teachers. Our Headmistress was at the station to see us off. She was angry with me for not wearing a school hat. Instead I had on one I'd bought with Bron's help at the St James's Street hat shop. 'A school hat-band will be posted to you and you will get a hat in France,' I was told. I didn't feel at all guilty, because my Aunt had said that of course I couldn't go to *Paris* in a school hat. On the train journey to Paris we opened the window of the steamy carriage but the angry guard came and shut it. As the rate of exchange, pounds and francs, was very much in our favour we were told not to discuss money in public places. We stayed in a luxurious students' hostel in the Boulevard Raspail; indulged in syrupy drinks in the Café du Dome; went to the Louvre and Fontainebleau, and for an evening drive in an open charabanc round Montmartre, where we all craned our necks to see the notorious 'Moulin Rouge', though heaven knows what we expected to see there.

At Versailles we bought postcards and tiny Napoleon hats. I remember a French woman glaring at us and saying, in French of course, to her companion: 'Those are little

Germans', but I said proudly, 'Madame, nous sommes anglaises', but it did little to improve her temper. At Fountainebleau after eating delicious omelettes and creamy *gateaux* we were directed to a shack in the back yard. The stench from a hole in the ground took away one's breath.

I bought presents for the family and a cheap grass hat at Galeries Lafayette, but the school hatband never arrived. We went to a performance of *Mignon* at the Opéra Comique and giggled when our popular little chaperone was accosted on the way back to the hostel. On the last evening a party of actors from the Comédie Française came to the Boulevard Raspail and acted passages from *Phèdre* by Racine. We all fell in love with the principal actor, who had blond curls, brown limbs and wore a short Greek tunic, and after the performance we shyly asked for his autograph.

During the General Strike in 1926, dressed in his beige Oxford bags, Merfyn drove a London bus. We saw him one day at Golders Green in his bus, which had BLONDES ONLY chalked boldly on its sides. When the strike was over and he was using the bus to take a girl home after a dance, an Inspector stopped him and said, 'You're a bit off your route, aren't you, sonny?'

At Jenny de la Mare's wedding Bronwen met a young Australian musician, who fell in love with her and pursued her ardently. He gave her an engagement ring with white sapphires which he had found in Australia.

I was studying hard for School Certificate. I knew that only if I passed could I escape from school: failure would mean staying on for another whole year.

Occasionally I went to London for the weekend; once I went with Bron and Harold, her fiancé, to a dance practice run by Jenny and Colin de la Mare and held in a Chelsea studio. At that time one could buy tubular artificial silk stockinette in rich colours; my favourite colour just then was green. Few seams were needed so Mother didn't take long to make me a bright green clinging dress with, oh joy, a two-inch edging of fur round the hem. I set out with Bron in my new slinky dress, my long strides restricted by the unyielding band of fur. The studio had a balcony overlooking the Thames. Harold and several friends from the Royal College of Music were already gathered round the pianist, whose name was Mark Anthony. Jenny de la Mare and her brother Colin were there, also Angus Morrison and Gavin Gordon-Brown, each later to make his name as pianist and composer of ballet music. Before long a young man asked me to dance. He had a slight limp, and looked like my idea of Pan, with fair loose curls from which budding horns might appear, and perhaps he limped because one elegant hoof had not quite changed back to a foot. I learned later that his name was Constant Lambert. I loved ballroom dancing and had never before had so many charming and handsome partners. On the balcony I chatted to a girl who told me she was training to be a dancer. I admired her dark hair, drawn back and knotted, her swirling dress of dark red Indian material, and her soft-blocked ballet shoes. As the evening wore on I became conscious of being more and more constricted about the calves and when I caught sight of myself in one of the wide looking-glasses, I realized that because of the weight of the fur my dress had 'dropped' several inches and the fur-edged hem was now nearing my ankles. I was covered in confusion and spent the rest of the night sitting on the balcony talking to my dancer friend.

Hubert and Kate Foss's friends were musicians, but they belonged to an older generation and to the so-called Bohemian world of which our family was on the fringe. Bronwen was now introduced to Harold's very different circle of musical friends. These young men were elegantly dressed, their shirts were specially made for them in Jermyn Street, their opera hats and leather-handled umbrellas were bought in St James's Street. They took girls to tea at Gunter's, off Park Lane, and dined at Rules in Maiden Lane. Their basement flats were sparsely and elegantly furnished, and there one drank Earl Grey tea with lemon from exquisite, fragile cups. They ordered Eccles cakes from Chester and florentines from Wigmore Street. Cigarettes were purchased from Freiburg & Treyer's bow-fronted shop in the Haymarket. Smoked salmon and exotic cheeses were carefully chosen at Fortnum & Mason. They told amusing stories of Henry Wood and Thomas Beecham, those legendary conductors, discussed foreign films, and went frequently to opera and ballet. They read Proust, Balzac, Stendhal, André Gide, and ignored Galsworthy, Priestley and Hugh Walpole. These sophisticated young men would not have been to see *Les Chauves Souris*, a Russian revue to which Mother took me, on Eleanor Farjeon's recommendation. I enjoyed the colour, the dancing and the balalaika, but even I squirmed at the *compère*, a suave, plump little man who introduced each turn in broken English, always ending with 'And these wan is by—myself—I am sore-r-ry!'

Bronnie and I went to a performance of 'A Mass of Life' at Queen's Hall and saw the composer, Delius, sitting motionless in a wheelchair, his saintly blind face turned towards the ceiling, his long white hands on his knees.

Margaret took her Girl Guides to join several other companies at a camp near Cooden on the south coast. It was a nightmarish experience: we hardly saw the sea but we certainly heard the crashing waves above the sound of wind and rain. We put up the tents with wet hands, the ropes stiff and hard, and filled our palliasses with straw. I was lucky to have my father's Jaeger sleeping-bag which had been returned from France after his death, but most of the other girls never got warm. Suet pudding and sausages were cooked in the open over a sullen fire of damp wood, and we washed up and dried plates and cups with soggy tea-cloths.

During the School Certificate exam term news came that Bron had had a serious operation at the Chelsea Hospital for Women. I went to see her and found her looking wanly beautiful. She told me of the attractive Russian houseman who delighted his patients by doing acrobatics on the metal cubicle bars between the beds; and of a member of the Diaghilev Ballet company who had been a fellow-patient.

As the School Certificate examination grew closer, I felt cocky about oral French, but grim about most of the other subjects, except perhaps English Literature. Quote and quote again our teacher had dinned into us; so we learned by heart parts of Bacon's essays and poems by Keats. *Macbeth* I knew well, and Chaucer's 'Prologue' I felt easy with. The essay question was 'Discuss fully secular life in Chaucer's England.' I smiled to myself; it was just up my street. I proceeded to write about the Prioress with her dainty table-manners, the Nun, the Pardoner and other characters who revealed the life of the clergy and the church in general. When I got home I showed the question paper to my aunt: she looked at those I had ticked. 'The Chaucer was lovely', I exulted.

'You wrote about the Wife of Bath and all her household details, the Tabard Inn, the Knight and the Squire—you must have enjoyed that,' said my aunt. My heart sank. 'No, I didn't. Surely secular means to do with the *Church*—like sect.' My aunt's face fell. 'But surely, lovey, you knew it means ordinary, worldly people as apart from the Church?' I felt my face going papery white. I had put my all into that essay and I had been completely on the wrong tack. 'Oh well', said my aunt, comfortingly, 'if you have a kind examiner and have done it well, perhaps he won't be too hard on you. Fancy not having had that word explained to you.' My aunt made me feel happier, as indeed she always did.

When exams were over one worked languidly and listened to the Upper Fifth's tales of tennis-parties, of driving to a dance in an open sports car, and of sly fun in the woods with boys from the nearby public school. In school we were asked what we wanted to do when we left. It was taken for granted that we would stay on to the sixth form and take Higher Certificate. There seemed to be little choice—nursing or teaching. I was quite certain I was not going to be a teacher; it put you on the shelf straight away, because at that time a married woman was debarred from teaching. I had no vocation for nursing. And I had no wish to stay on for another year.

We in the Upper Fifth were asked to choose a book as an end-of-the-year prize. I chose Walter de la Mare's *Memoirs of a Midget*—but I was presented with a social history of the eighteenth century; it had some amusing pictures, but several years later I gave it to Harry Batsford for the publisher's reference library.

At last news came that I had passed School Certificate. I must have had a kindly examiner for my Chaucer essay, as I had gained a Credit for Literature and the necessary number of marks on other papers. It was decided that I should go to my uncle's office in Victoria Street where he was a Consulting Engineer. His assistant would teach me shorthand; I would open the letters, answer the telephone, nip out to the Army & Navy Stores for my uncle's lunch-time sandwiches, and undertake research into gas and water engineering Parliamentary Bills. As a final treat for gaining School Certificate, I was to go to Champery in Switzerland with my aunt, uncle and cousin for four weeks in August.

In those days the Automobile Association produced the most detailed and foolproof itinerary for motorists going abroad, beginning with how to get your car away from the docks and on to the right road. You mentioned to the AA that you would like to pass through certain towns and villages, avoiding as much as possible crowded main roads, and you were sent a bound volume of typed pages giving minute instructions, such as 'Turn left 100 yards after passing a windmill—there is a church worth looking at in the market town 9 miles ahead'. The AA would recommend the best *pension* or hotel, and point out restaurants along the route which specialized in particular delicacies.

My uncle always drank champagne on Channel crossings as an insurance against sea-sickness. His wife and daughter joined him, but I leaned on the rails, watching the ship's wake and imagining all my schooldays churned away for ever in the dizzy foam.

We bowled along the dusty roads from Calais, seeing the acres of white crosses of the war dead, and further on the acres of black crosses which marked German graves. We ate delicious food and drank the wine of the district or Malvern water; my uncle had taught me never to drink tap water as drains in France weren't all they should be. When we stopped at a country *pension* for the night, while we sat in the car my aunt went in to look at the bedrooms, stripping back the bedclothes in full view of *la patronne* to make sure there were no signs of bugs. This ritual seemed to be expected of the eccentric English and caused no offence though I found it desperately embarrassing.

There was no road up to one hotel, only a winding cobbled path for donkeys. Our luggage was winched up by block and tackle from an upstairs window. We looked at churches and cathedrals, and eventually climbed through the Alps to the great chalet-like hotel at Champery with its

view of the sharp peaks of the Dents du Midi. The sound of
the cow-bells, the heady air, the snowy peaks and the songs
of the militia camping nearby were magical. It was the first
time I had stayed in a large hotel, with a ballroom; I had
brought several evening dresses with me and a number of
new cotton ones for day-time. In 1927 most dresses had
their waist-seams at finger-tip length and the short skirt
came just to the knees.

I fell in love at once with a young Swiss dance professional,
who was also the tennis coach. He danced with Margaret
and me on the first evening, as we were newcomers. Joseph
was fair, solemn and courteous, and danced with me as much
as he could. This was lucky, for my only other partner was
my uncle. I made friends with the Austrian band leader and
occasionally he let me play the drums for a tango. On
Joseph's evening off we danced to the gramophone in an
empty bar and drank sweet white wine. I was very ill in the
night and have never drunk white wine since. In the afternoons we danced on a raised platform near the tennis courts,
or watched the tennis. Margaret played well and had made
friends with two young couples. I was fascinated by the way
the balls sailed so high in the light air. We went for walks
up mountain paths, longing to drink the ice-cold water from
the rushing streams—but notices proclaimed that the water
was contaminated. This puzzled me, but Margaret said that
higher up there was a large sanatorium for tubercular patients.

Mother joined us for a few days. She had been staying at
Vevey with one of her former pupils at Steep. She was full
of plans for Bron's second wedding, though apprehensive
about Harold who had only casual jobs as accompanist to
professional singers. Mother's book, *As It Was*, was soon to
be published.

During the drive home through France I hummed the airs
of the two tangos which the band had played every night

and which I had danced with Joseph—in case I should ever forget them. That was the most romantic, carefree and happy time of my life—for at last I felt that I did something well and that I was liked.

'Here on the height of our girlhood's dreamland
Life's way before us lies.'

Soon I would start work in my uncle's office.

Edward in 1914 with Myfanwy and Tommy Dodd

Edward, middle row, second from left, at army training camp

Myfanwy, aged 12

Granny Thomas, about 1910

Bronwen, aged 12

Helen, 1914

Merfyn, late 1918

Myfanwy, Belle and Di at Otford, 1919

Bronwen, Myfanwy and Merfyn, early 1918

Helen, Auntie Florrie, Dick and Uncle Ernest at Seaford, 1920